23 Female Entrepreneurs
Their Journeys To *Success*

THE RÎSE
OF THE FEMALE ENTREPRENEUR

Discover the resilience, passion, and unwavering
determination that fueled their ascent to success

Lyndsey Meredith & Co

Copyright© 2024 Lyndsey Meredith

By Pro Publishing House

ISBN: 9798883512727

The following chapters are Lyndsey Meredith & Co's intellectual property and the stories of the individuals. All rights reserved. No part of this book may be reproduced or modified in any form, including photocopying, recording, or by information storage and retrieval system, without written permission from the publisher/author. All rights reserved.

Legal Notice:

This book is for personal use only. You cannot amend, distribute, sell, use, quote or paraphrase any part of this book's content without the author's or copyright owner's consent. Legal action will be pursued if this is breached. The information provided herein is stated to be truthful and consistent in that any liability, in terms of inattention or otherwise, by any usage or abuse of any policies, processes, or directions contained within is the solitary and utter responsibility of the recipient reader. Under no circumstances will any legal responsibility or blame be held against the publisher for any reparation, damages, or monetary loss due to the information herein, either directly or indirectly.

Disclaimer Notice:

All Authors in this book are not doctors or providing medical recommendations; this book is not providing medical advice; it is intended for informational purposes only. It is not a substitute for professional medical advice, diagnosis or treatment. Never ignore professional medical advice in seeking treatment. Every attempt has been made to provide accurate, up-to-date, reliable, and complete information. No warranties of any kind are expressed or implied. Readers acknowledge that the author is not engaging in the rendering of legal, financial, medical or professional advice.

By reading this document, the reader agrees that under no circumstances are we responsible for any losses, direct or indirect, which are incurred as a result of the use of the information contained within this document, including, but not limited to, errors, omissions, or inaccuracies.

These stories are written by real women in their own words.

Book Cover Design: Tracey Munro

DEDICATION

This book is dedicated to my Nannan Beryl Hodgson who taught me that when you do what you love it will never really feel like work. She was a true female entrepreneur who owned and ran her pub "The Keel Inn" in Barnsley for over 52 years from 1968 until her death in 2021.

Nannan was a huge inspiration to my sisters and I, and many others in her community and is a fantastic example of a woman that built and ran her own business through hard times with unwavering belief. It wasn't just a business; it was her life and she truly loved it.

On this International Women's Day 2024 I want to celebrate her and all female entrepreneurs around the world who are building their own businesses no matter what it takes.

THE RISE OF THE FEMALE ENTREPRENEUR

CONTENTS

FORWARD — **Page 7**

CHAPTER 1: Gillian Devine — **Page 11**

CHAPTER 2: Lyndsey Meredith — **Page 23**

CHAPTER 3: Anna Anderson — **Page 39**

CHAPTER 4: Karen Deulofeu — **Page 51**

CHAPTER 5: Andrea Rainsford — **Page 67**

CHAPTER 6: Dorothy Norris — **Page 79**

CHAPTER 7: Janey Holliday — **Page 91**

CHAPTER 8: Charlotte Dover — **Page 103**

CHAPTER 9: Aneeta Marshall Law — **Page 117**

CHAPTER 10: Gemma Howorth — **Page 129**

CHAPTER 11: Jenna Richardson — **Page 145**

CHAPTER 12: Joanna Oakley — **Page 157**

CHAPTER 13: Jessica Harvey — **Page 171**

CHAPTER 14: Laura Davies — **Page 183**

CHAPTER 15: Jo Douglas — **Page 199**

CHAPTER 16: Jo Mould — **Page 211**

CHAPTER 17: Ali Braid — **Page 227**

CHAPTER 18: Kathleen Van den Berghe — **Page 239**

CHAPTER 19: Kaytie Chambers — **Page 251**

CHAPTER 20: Alvina Menzies — **Page 261**

CHAPTER 21: Kate Gerald — **Page 275**

CHAPTER 22: Linda Scerri — **Page 289**

CHAPTER 23: Sarah Makinde — **Page 301**

ACKNOWLEGEMENTS — **Page 311**

FORWORD
By Lyndsey Meredith
LinkedIn & Visibility Coach, 14-year business owner and MUM

It has been my pleasure and my privilege to bring together the amazing and inspiring women whose stories are featured in this book. This book is a celebration of their journeys, their achievements, and the impact that they are having upon the world.

Ever since my college days, when I first studied sociology and learned more about the glass ceiling for women, I have been hugely passionate about women achieving their potential.

I firmly believe that women don't need to fight for a seat at the table, for we are perfectly capable of building our own, and I have made it my mission to instill this in my daughter as she grows up.

As you read this book, you will notice that every one of these women has had hard times and had to make hard decisions. However, it has often been in the hard times that they have discovered their true potential.

THE RISE OF THE FEMALE ENTREPRENEUR

We are all truly capable of anything, no matter where we started. Each woman in this book has been on a unique journey and has their own unique story to tell in their own words. My hope is that you will be inspired- wherever you are now- to take control of YOUR own story.

We decided to publish this book to coincide with International Women's Day 2024, and all proceeds from its sales will go to "Women Supporting Women" which is part of the Princes Trust, which we as authors have chosen as a collective.

You will find my own story in Chapter 2.

Wishing you every success on your own journey,

Lyndsey x

> *"Nothing is impossible, the word itself says I'm possible!"*
>
> **...Audrey Hepburn**

THE RISE OF THE FEMALE ENTREPRENEUR

CHAPTER 1
Gillian Devine
Brand Photography Specialist & Photographers Business Coach and Mentor

Pinch me! Because right now, I am literally living my dream. I'm running both my businesses, one as a business coach and mentor to photographers and business owners, and secondly as a brand photographer from my dream home on the Costa Blanca, Spain. I have huge amounts of joy and make great money in both. I love coaching and inspiring thousands of amazing photographers to successfully market and monetise their craft. I also adore working as a brand photographer, helping other business owners be more visible and thrive. Life is the best! I love Spain and my work, and I am married to my absolute soulmate. But getting here hasn't been easy. In this chapter, I want to share with you my story and the learnings that have enabled me to rise as a successful entrepreneur. So buckle up!

Back in 2010, I was living alone in a rather spooky Victorian house near Worsley, Greater Manchester, when there was a knock at the door one morning. I opened it to find two police officers on the doorstep asking me to step inside. A million thoughts rushed through my head. Had something awful happened to a family member? Had someone been hurt or killed?

They entered the long, dark hallway and began talking about the theft of a car. My car, it seemed, was a Mercedes SLK, which, seconds before, I had seen parked on the driveway where I'd left it. There had clearly been a mix-up.

With some relief I interrupted to explain that the car was perfectly safe – "Look, I have the keys". But they didn't seem to listen. Instead, I was being told, in a rather severe tone, that car theft is a very serious offence. It sounded like I was being accused. It sounded like I was about to be arrested! And then the penny dropped. No! Surely he wouldn't do that.

Apparently, my ex-husband reported that I had stolen the Merc – the car he had given me as a birthday present two years previously. "But it's mine," I insisted. "It's in my name, I have the paperwork." "No, you don't," came the reply. "It's in your husband's name, and strictly speaking, you've stolen it." I immediately burst into tears…

None of this should have come as a surprise. After years of physical and emotional abuse from my ex, I was also left in a huge amount of debt that I only discovered when I finally escaped. The equity I thought we had in the jointly owned house was gone, my financial security disappeared, and it was only thanks to the 'Bank of Dad' that I had managed to afford a rental home to move into.

At the time of this police visit, my emotional state, confidence and self-worth were already on the floor, and I was struggling to keep my head above water in the running of my business. In the end, I just had to drop the keys through the letterbox of my old home. But I was left trying to run a business and hold down a second job without my own means of transport, as well as facing severe financial difficulty. It was a particularly low point. I was in my mid-30s, facing divorce, severely in debt, without a car and borrowing money from my father. How had it come to this? How was I going to run my photography business and get to weddings and shoots without transport?

I hadn't always been a photographer. I had come out of university with a geography degree and then completely pivoted to a corporate career in sales and marketing. It was thanks to my lovely father-in-law Vincent that I got a break into running my own business. Vincent was a professional photographer, and I'd often act as his assistant on weekend wedding shoots, organising people into groups, fluffing the bride's veil, and carrying the kit. I loved it!

As time went by, I became more and more involved, second shooting for Vincent and doing a few shots of my own at the weekends. When Vincent retired, he decided to hand the business over to me, saying that he was sure I was capable. It was rather bewildering to suddenly think of myself as a business owner, but Vincent really gave me belief in myself.

Running my own business was wonderful. I loved capturing memories for my clients to treasure. Whether it was a wedding day, a pregnancy, the birth of a first child or even a business story, I was passionate about it.

But now, after the trauma of a nasty divorce, the debt revelations and my ex's continued harassment, I had lost all confidence. I had stopped marketing the business and ceased looking for work, so, inevitably, the jobs weren't coming in. The business I had been so enthusiastic about was slowly dying, and I was becoming ever more reliant on the little income I was getting from a part-time job as a beauty salon receptionist. I was completely lost.

Taking action

I knew I needed to get a grip and pull myself out of this hole, and a real turning point came when I read "Get Rich, Lucy Bitch!" by Denise Duffield-Thomas. It was a lightbulb moment as the author inspired and motivated me to develop a strong money mindset, take action, and rebuild my business step by step. I still have my copy of that book, and it's battered with lots of notes and turned-down pages.

I followed her advice, and I began to take action. At first, it was just the simple things: refreshing my pricing to reflect my work, getting back on social media, and marketing myself again. I realised I couldn't let my past dictate my future, I was worthy, and I could achieve anything I set my mind to. I became a self-development junkie, absorbing videos, books, and any content from people like Mel Robbins, Nick Vujicic, Louise Hay, and Tony Robbins, and I started to feel more empowered and in control.

Well-known motivational speaker Tony Robbins said that there are two things that will drive you forward: inspiration and desperation. Well, I had both. I was inspired by Denise Duffield Thomas and other successful business owners, and I was also desperate to pay my bills, have some financial stability and pay my father back!

I worked hard and smart to grow my business on my own, and I was so proud of my progress. My business was growing again, and I was profitable again, but it came to a point where I felt I needed further help, particularly with my marketing and business strategies. So I decided it was time to get some guidance, and I invested all the money I had left, scrimped and saved together, £6,000 in total, into a business coach. At the time, I had just started a relationship with my future husband, Lee, and he was astonished that I'd give such a sizeable chunk of money to a complete stranger. But it was a risk worth taking I thought. Yes, I was nervous and scared, but I knew that to scale and grow my business, I needed to take on someone who would guide and support me and someone who was already achieving what I wanted to achieve. It was the right decision...through that mix of inspiration and desperation to make it work, I made that £6,000 back within five weeks by applying what my mentor taught me.

That is definitely one of the keys to success, the willingness to try and apply something different, and to invest in yourself and your business. I went into it with a 'can do' attitude, willing to apply any of the strategies the coach showed me to scale my business. If he had instructed me to hop around the room on one foot, I would have done it because I needed it to work! I followed his guidance to the letter, even though sometimes I felt fear. For instance, when he told me that instead of £300, I should charge £1000 for a photography package, "people aren't going to pay that," I thought. But I was wrong.

The right money mindset

What I was continuing to understand more and more is that if you want to run a successful, profitable business, you have to have a strong money mindset. You have to be continually conscious of any negative thoughts, feelings or actions concerning money. A lot of us have limiting beliefs around money, and this can stem from many places, such as our upbringing and childhood (were you ever told "money doesn't grow on trees!") and also in the media where rich people are usually portrayed as evil and scheming.

Mentoring other photographers and seeing their reactions is always interesting when I suggest it's time for a price increase. If their instant response is "I'm not good enough," or "I haven't been doing it long enough," or "the people around here won't pay that", then I gently tell them to think again. There are clients for our services at every price point level, it's just about getting your marketing right. I used to live in one of the most disadvantaged areas in the north of England, but I didn't let that dictate my business and marketing strategies or my price points. I was charging premium photography prices, providing wonderful memorable experiences for all my clients, and building a hugely successful and profitable photography business. It worked because I was marketing to the right people in the right way.

In the past, I had been naive in allowing others to manage my money, and it negatively impacted me. I promised myself I would take full control of my finances going forward. These days, I love number crunching. Having a strong set of financial goals and a plan on how to achieve them is one of the key routes to success. Vague and airy-fairy monetary ambitions will only ever deliver vague and airy-fairy results.

Making dreams a reality

Fast forward in time, my businesses are now thriving, and I had a new dream. I wanted to live in the sun.

There were a few pivotal moments to making this decision. The first came when we rented a very cold, draughty, but really pretty cottage. Snowed in one winter, with drifts above head height I had to cancel all my photography shoots while Lee couldn't get home from work. Cuddled up on the sofa, trying to keep warm, I binge-watched "A Place in the Sun." "Arrhaa," I thought! "Now there is an idea."

I began to research property prices and the areas I wanted to live in. I attended A Place in the Sun events and spoke with exhibitors and traders, trying to get a fuller understanding of how to make my dream come true. I started visiting different areas of Spain and speaking to people who were already living out there. I am a firm believer that if you want change, you have to be the change. There is no point just dreaming these things, and not doing anything about it! We have to take action, do the do! Make things happen for yourself.

The second pivotal moment came one sunny Saturday when Lee and I were residing in our tiny flat in Oldham. The property didn't have a garden or balcony, so the only place I could catch some rays was by setting up a deckchair in the car park. I closed my eyes, and I visualised myself not in an Oldham car park but sitting beside a villa – my own villa – on Spain's Costa Blanca. So, I decided to make that vision a reality. I wanted to take Costa-del-Car-Parkio and make it Costa Blanca!

Lee was now completely on board with the idea of living in Spain, and we continued our search for the perfect property together. (Another tip for you: if you want something, like really want it, become super passionate, determined and persuasive. Project all your energy into it! Because surely your dreams deserve it!)

The journey wasn't smooth. The first three houses we intended to buy in Spain fell through, and there were lots of frustrations. However, we eventually found our dream villa on the Costa Blanca, just as I had envisioned on that sunny Saturday in Oldham's Costa Del Car Parkio.

(Another tip - don't let bumps in the road deviate you from your dreams and goals. I remember crying about the collapse of the first dream house we wanted in Spain. I was devastated! I had chalked all my furniture out on the floor when the purchase fell through. I could have given up, but I didn't. Just a bump in the road, I convinced myself, there must be a better house out there waiting for me. And there was)

I believe I was able to manifest my dream because I had a clear vision of what I wanted, I had worked out a plan on how to make it happen, and I took action. This is something I always emphasise to the photographers I work with. I ask them to create visual representations of what they want to achieve in the form of dream and goal boards, as well as mapping out their desired monetary ambitions and timescales for growth, and then we make these a reality through taking action. Their dream board and their financial goal spreadsheet, these things become the spring boards for taking steps, taking action, to make a goal a reality.

Seizing opportunities

I have been in the photography business for 18 years as of today, and I've worked with some wonderful people, visited some fabulous locations and created a varied body of work that I'm truly proud of—expanding my business to run mentorship and business coaching programmes for other photographers felt so natural.

The roots of this go back to my own group coaching sessions with my own then mentor when I was in a room of perhaps 25 to 30 photographers. As I was one of the most successful photographers there, many of the mentees were coming to me for additional guidance and advice, and I just loved helping them.

When this mentorship programme closed, a lot of my group went into a flat panic. They came to me and told me they wanted me to start coaching them because I'd been helping them anyway. So, I began offering one-to-one business and marketing mentoring sessions for photographers. I grabbed the opportunity to help others build their own profitable and successful photography businesses and the start of my mentoring business began. I also took on another business coach myself to help form an online business and marketing school for photographers. The opportunity to help other photographers could have passed me by if I hadn't taken action, if I had let fear or imposter syndrome get in my way.

I went on to launch my online business and marketing school, the Rich Tog Academy. 'Tog' is short for photographer, and my aim is to make them rich – 'rich' in terms of happiness, confidence and fulfilment, as well as monetary wealth.

So here I am now, running two successful and profitable businesses that bring me masses of joy. I am now a specialist brand photographer working to help businesses be visible and thrive. In my coaching business, I mentor and teach thousands of other photographers in my online courses and programmes, my 1-2-1 coaching packages and luxury retreats over here in Spain. I work with photographers all over the world, from start-ups to established photographers and those working in all the different genres.

I also love to give back to the photography community, so I have also created lots of free resources (links at the bottom of this chapter) and speak on stage at conferences and events. I regularly fly back and forth between the UK and Spain, serving clients in both businesses.

As I said, I am literally living my version of success, my dream. And if I can do it, then so can you.

Work on you

One of the most important things you can do for yourself, and your life and business is to dedicate time to self-care and self-development. You may think, 'What in the jam sandwich is meditating every morning and writing down my thoughts and goals in a book got to do with business?' But you would be surprised. The most successful people in the world are working on themselves daily, on their minds, their body, and their learning. I teach the importance of working on yourself and looking after yourself. We are only here once, right? So we need to squeeze the juice out of every moment.

Learn from and lift others

Another thing I stress is to mix with other inspirational, aspirational, positive and uplifting souls. People who you love to be around, who give you a boost and inspire you to achieve your dreams. I am hugely careful about who I mix my energy with, but I am lucky enough to have a fantastic circle of friends, students, mentees and a wonderfully inspiring group of female entrepreneur colleagues, whose company I enjoy and benefit from. A gorgeous friend of mine has a favourite saying, "We rise by lifting others", which is something I believe and aim to practise.

I would love to help you!

I honestly hope I have inspired you to see that anything is possible for any of us if we simply have belief, decide what we want and take action towards it.

If you are a photographer, I would love to help you in your business.
I have online business and marketing courses and programmes for photographers, and I continue to provide one-to-one mentoring too, both in person and online. I also run Rich Tog Retreats in Spain, where photographers come for a luxury retreat mixed with business and marketing strategy sessions, all under the Spanish sunshine.

Having worked in all these genres myself, I would definitely say that brand photography is my favourite genre for 'togs' to go into, and it's definitely been the favourite for me. It gives a better work-life balance (weddings, for instance, require a lot of weekend work); it tends to be a little more refined (very different from newborns, which involves being in a hot, sweaty room and potentially dealing with poop). And, crucially, it's more profitable because it's mainly digital delivery, and businesses are happy to invest in what is essential for their business growth. For me, brand photography is 3-hour mid week shoots, a light edit, supporting businesses that invest with ease, helping them be more visible and market effectively. Gone are the days of working weekends, missing out on family and friend time, and then editing late into the night.

All businesses need brand photography services, from florists to estate agents, and accountancy firms to online therapists. Brand photography provides all the imagery they need for social media, websites and marketing materials. So, as a brand photographer, you get to choose who you want to work with, from the tiniest local companies through to big international corporations. There are so many reasons why I love working in this field, and I am constantly educating other photographers on the benefits of it, moving into this area either alongside their other genres, for additional income, or as a specialist like me.

If you're a photographer and you'd like help generating leads and enquiries into your business, then I would love to offer you access to my free online Marketing Masterclass. In these hour-long live and interactive classes, I will bring clarity to some key marketing principles and provide advice on putting these in place to ensure your business flourishes. Easily actionable tasks, activities and strategies to boost your presence, attract the right clients and bring in the money you deserve. With a healthy dose of positive energy and motivation, I know I will inspire and help you on the path to create your own dream business.

I would also be delighted to offer you complimentary access to my five-day mini course, all online, with daily live marketing sessions and mini tasks for you to do to help your business grow.

Check these links to find out more about any of these free resources.
Website: www.gilliandevine.com/masterclass
Website: www.gilliandevine.com/5-day

I genuinely wish you all the luck in the world with your own dreams and goals. I believe in you. Now go believe in yourself and start taking action.

Much love, Gill x

CHAPTER 2
Lyndsey Meredith
LinkedIn & Visibility Coach

The Early Years

I was born in February 1984, one half of a set of identical twins. Myself and my twin sister Louise also had an older sister Nicola, who was two years eight months older than us. My parents came from a working-class background in Barnsley, where they met as children. My mum was a nursery assistant, and my dad worked for a bank.

My dad was successful in a very traditional way. He had a profession for life. Starting on the banking counter in Barnsley at 16 years old, he worked for the same bank his whole working life, working his way up into Senior Positions until he retired at 56. He had a stable and reliable career with a final salary pension. We moved for his job, settling in Darlington in the North East when I was 2 ½, and this is where we spent most of our childhood. It was a great childhood. My mum was a fantastic mum, even getting a job in the nursery that we went to. My dad worked hard and instilled a strong work ethic in us. Family and family values were important.

We left Darlington and moved to Bramhall in the North West when I was 12. My dad had got a promotion and now worked at the head office of the bank in Manchester. Moving a term into year seven and leaving behind everything and everyone we had grown up with was difficult but also exciting and changed the direction of my life. Manchester was only 10 minutes away on the train, and I felt as though a whole new world had opened up to me. I had left childhood behind and embraced my teenage years with new horizons. I worked hard at school, followed the rules, did everything that I was supposed to and did well in my GCSE's and A Levels.

At 18, I was offered a place at Manchester University to study Sociology. I chose Sociology as I had studied it at college and was fascinated by the study of people and societies and how and why they act as they do. I loved University. Being surrounded by knowledge and history was such a privilege. I would sit in the John Rylands Library and literally just breathe in the smell of the books. This is where my love of gaining knowledge really blossomed and is something that I would take with me on my entrepreneurial journey.

The start of my career

I've had a job since I was 14 years old. Firstly, in a local fruit shop, then in a local garden centre, and finally in 2 local bars whilst at university, but I hadn't really got much of an idea about what I wanted to do when I "grew up."

During the long break in my 2nd year at university, my dad got me a job in the Head Office of his bank. I worked on a different floor to him, processing cheques and debits. I learned several things whilst working at the bank that summer, but the most important one was that if you are in excruciating pain and can't get up from your desk that you probably have appendicitis and should get the hell home instead of worrying about what people would think!! I had literally waited until my appendix was about to burst before asking to go home as I was "at work."

I returned to the bank two weeks after having my appendix out with a brand-new scar. In reality, I could have spent the last few weeks of the holidays continuing to recover at home. What I didn't realise at the time was that I had a deeply rooted work ethic instilled in me, borne from having watched the commitment Dad gave to the bank all of those years. And I am very glad that I did go back because a chance encounter changed everything.

It was busy at the bank, and I wasn't the only member of staff hired just for the summer. The bank had hired "temps" from a local recruitment agency. I had never heard of a recruitment agency before this, and so when the recruitment consultant came into the office to check on her staff and we got chatting, I asked her a lot of questions.

She spent her days talking to people, interviewing candidates, matching them with businesses and checking that everyone was happy. She had a job that was all about people, was varied and seemed fun. With my background in sociology this really resonated with me, and I decided that when I graduated, I was going to become a Recruitment Consultant. I'm one of the only people that I have ever met who planned on being a Recruitment Consultant and didn't just "fall into it!"

I graduated with a 2:1 degree, full of excitement for what came next, but I soon found that it wasn't as easy as just deciding that I wanted to be a "Recruitment Consultant." There were lots of recruitment jobs out there, but they were not looking for graduates. They were looking for people with sales experience. I soon realised that my shiny new degree didn't actually give me a leg up in my chosen industry at all. I applied for many recruitment jobs- all stating that they wanted sales experience with a cover letter stating, "I don't have any sales experience. However," and finally, one day at the end of the summer, I got a reply from a small independent recruitment agency called NES who were willing to give me a chance.

I started from the bottom, making "cold" calls to local businesses to generate new opportunities for our candidates. It was hard work, but I loved it, and that £14,000 salary felt like a million!

I had a natural sales ability and resilience. If one person said no, I just moved on to the next. After a year at NES, I realised that my ambitions lay beyond the small agency and the cocoon that it had provided and moved on with their blessing to work for a large national agency at their offices in Stockport.

The "Coup" that changed everything

About two years into my employment, I went in one morning to find that the manager and all of the senior staff had left overnight with some senior managers in a bit of a "coup." It was to be business as usual until we got further word. That word came a few days later when the MD of the national business arrived at our office. He was keen to reassure us and met with each of us personally. Before he left the branch that day, he told me that they were going to advertise the Branch Manager vacancy and that he thought that I should apply for it. My reaction was, "What? Me?" I went home to my now husband dumbfounded that he would think that a 24-year-old with three years of recruitment and no management experience would be a good prospect. My husband's response was that he had obviously seen something in me, so why not see where it went?

So, a week later, I found myself on a train to London, where I was asked to present a business plan for my plans for the Stockport office to the MD at the Baker Street office. I was terrified!! I had no clue what I was doing and felt totally out of my comfort zone. So how did it go? I left Baker Street with a job offer, an £8k pay rise, a company car allowance and still no clue what I was doing!!

I returned to the office to make the announcement that I- the most recent hire in the office and by far the youngest employee- was now their boss. Well, you can imagine how that went down…

The next 12 months were a baptism by fire. I was thrown into the world of profit and loss accounts and management meetings, staff issues and stresses. It was by far the most stressful period of my career, but I am forever grateful for it. What that MD did in throwing me in at the deep end to sink or swim made me who I am today. I was no longer a loyal employee that followed someone else's direction. It was my responsibility to set the direction and get everyone's buy-in. I started to understand how business worked at a whole new level. Each branch essentially operated as its own business, and I was in charge and tasked with running it as my own business. When it came to either sinking or swimming…I swam.

As I moved into the second year of running the office and we had moved to a more even keel, the 2008 recession started to bite, and the things that had always worked just didn't work anymore. It was my job to chart a new course and try new things. This agility, when things got tough, would go on to make me the business owner that I am today, and so whilst the recession was very hard on the recruitment industry and my branch eventually closed, leaving us redundant, I am very grateful for everything that I learned on that journey.

At 25 and newly redundant from my Branch Manager role, I was "displaced" in the business and asked to cover the Stockport patch from the Altrincham office. I was a consultant again, and so I decided to move to an independent recruitment agency in Salford as their Business Development Manager. This allowed me flexibility and autonomy over my diary, and I enjoyed a very successful six months there. I soon learned that I could be successful anywhere. With my newfound knowledge I learned from running a recruitment business and getting to know the owners of the Salford business, I soon realised that I had the ability and knowledge to run my OWN business.

Working for someone else just wasn't going to cut it anymore. I shared how I was feeling with my bosses. They totally understood, and I left with their blessing.

So, in May 2010, I left my job, got married and went on a 2 ½ week honeymoon to Thailand. On the 1st of June 2010, I started my own recruitment agency, and my entrepreneurial journey was born.

Doing It For Myself

I worked hard and gained clients quickly, generating £4k in revenue in my first month. Then came the summer and the recruitment "lull", and there were a few months of £0 revenue. But I wasn't in this for the short term. I had invested £5k of my own money into this venture. My costs were super low, and I didn't plan on paying myself until I made a profit. Thankfully, I had my husband's support, and our personal outgoings were low. I had nothing to lose and everything to gain. I made £22,000 in revenue that year. It was tiny compared to my recruitment branch. But it wasn't about the money. I had proven that I could run my own business and make a profit in my very first year of trading. My accountant at the time was a sweet old man who told me when reading those accounts, "You have a business", and I couldn't have been prouder.

I worked from home for the first year, and then I rented an office locally for the next few years. With clients and an office, I felt like I was running a proper business and loved it. But I was getting to my late 20s and feeling my biological clock start to tick. I started thinking about what would happen to my business if I took time off for maternity leave, as it solely relied on me and panic set in. During the most successful revenue year of my business so far, I closed it down. If I wanted to have a baby before I was 30, I needed a "real" job.

I quickly found a role as a BDM for a start-up company who relished my experience as a business owner, as it meant that I could talk to their clients on a different level to the other applicants. They gave me an amazing salary, bonus and car allowance. I did well straight away and was earning great money with lots of autonomy. However, I quickly realised I had made a mistake.

No amount of money or security could take away the fact that I now had a "boss", and the business that I was making money for wasn't mine! Before I could decide what to do, I fell pregnant with my daughter, and that stability was even more important, so I just focused on being as successful as possible in the run up to her being born. This wasn't always easy, as I was very sick with hyperemesis, but I showed up every day and worked hard- just as my dad had always taught me. I would decide what to do after my daughter was born. In the end, the decision was made for me as whilst I was on maternity leave, the business I had been working for went into insolvency. I was redundant again. And just like before, when I was made redundant, this was the catalyst for what happened next, and I am forever grateful.

New Beginnings

I was now 30 years old, a first-time mother and unemployed for the first time since I was 14. That maternity leave- as I know has happened for so many others- put everything into perspective for me. I finally had the time and space to think about what I really wanted and what I wanted my life to look like for me, my daughter and our family. I was a mum who had the ability and the skills to control my own destiny. I could build a business around my daughter and her needs. She could have the childhood that I had where my mum never missed a drop-off or a pickup, AND I could run a business, control my own income and my own destiny.

And so I did. When Izzy was nine months old, I returned to work. I restarted my recruitment agency, having learned from all of the previous lessons with a renewed sense of purpose. I wasn't just doing this for me anymore. It wasn't just about money. It was for my daughter and to give her an amazing life, and with that in mind, I couldn't fail.

Over the next seven years, I built a profitable business from home. I have never missed a pickup or a drop-off. I have been on every school trip and attended every school event. She doesn't even need to ask; she just knows that I will be there, and that is my biggest achievement.

To all intents and purposes, I have been a full-time mother AND a full-time business owner. My daughter has had the best of me, and so has my business. How? Because I built the business around her and for her. And just as important, she has grown up knowing that she doesn't have to wait for a seat at the table- she can build her own table.

It got to 2019, and my daughter was at school, and my business was doing well. It gave me total flexibility, but in all honesty, I had fallen out of love with recruitment. Over the previous few years, I had started mentoring others who wanted advice on starting their own recruitment agencies, and I started to love doing this more than recruitment. It became my outlet and my passion.

I started a Facebook Group called "The Female Recruiter" to support others and started to question whether I was now in the right business or whether now was the time to make a change. I had started and grown one business successfully, so I was fully confident that I could start another. But my recruitment business was doing well, and I was afraid of making that change even though I knew in my gut that it was the right thing to do.

Then COVID hit, and everything changed anyway

Those businesses that I had been helping? They needed my help more than ever. The recruitment industry literally disappeared overnight. Back then, as you know, we lived day-to-day. No one knew what was going to happen. So I just focused on getting up every day, home schooling Izzy and getting through the day. My husband Paul had to continue to go to work as his factory was making essential equipment for government test centres, and I was always worried that he would get ill.

Whilst in lockdown, an opportunity presented itself. It was a period of time when I literally couldn't work because all of my clients were closed, and more importantly, I had time to think. What if I used this time to make that change? So, I did. I signed up for a Coaching qualification, and whilst Izzy did her home school lessons, I sat next to her and did my own schoolwork!

As the world started to open up again, so did mine. I launched my coaching business, and I have never looked back. It felt so natural and aligned, and I loved being able to directly see the impact that I was making on my clients. In the beginning, I acted as a general business mentor to recruitment businesses getting back on their feet after the covid lockdowns. All of my work was done via Zoom, and this opened up the opportunity to work with clients all over the world, ranging from the UK, and US to Australia and even Argentina.

The thing that I loved to coach on the most was sales & marketing. I quickly realised that just as this had been something that I had enjoyed in my own recruitment business, this was where my passion lay in my coaching business.

You Are Your Own Brand

At the time, the concept of Personal Branding was starting to gain more attention. Personal branding is the act of marketing yourself as the face of your business. People buy from people, meaning that they buy into the business owner first and then into their business.

I realised that I had actually been a pioneer of personal branding in my recruitment business without even realising it, and this had led to my success. When I first started my recruitment business, it was important for me to do things differently from my local competitors. Back then, in 2010, all recruiters did the majority of their sales and new business development via cold calling. I knew that this approach often garnered recruiters a bad reputation and made potential prospects feel uncomfortable, and so I decided to do the opposite. I was an early adopter of the business social media platform LinkedIn. At a time when everyone else was using it as a CV site, I was using it to build my reputation and gain clients for my recruitment business.

I didn't realise at the time that I was building a personal brand, but looking back; this is the very thing that allowed me to build my recruitment business so successfully in a way that felt good for myself and my clients. It was personal YET scalable and allowed my prospects to get to know me from afar without ever feeling as though they were in an uncomfortable sales situation.

Post-covid, the world of recruitment had changed, and this meant that the business owners that I was working with had to change and adapt how they did things too. People no longer answered their phones like they used to. A lot of people didn't work from the office anymore, and switchboards didn't give out mobile numbers. In short… cold calling didn't work as well anymore, and they had to find new methods of doing things.

So, I started teaching my clients how to build a personal brand on LinkedIn. It was a no-brainer. For most recruitment businesses, LinkedIn could act as a database of all of their potential ideal clients. They were all on there, just waiting for them.

Sales changed post covid. People didn't want to be "sold" to. They craved connection and real relationships, so it was not enough for my recruitment owner clients to spam them on LinkedIn. Therefore, it was the perfect time for me to teach them how to use LinkedIn to build a personal brand that built genuine connections and produced genuine results with clients that CHOSE to work with them. This led to more business from the right people. I soon had lots of clients, both from referrals from my existing clients and my own growing personal brand on LinkedIn, and this is how I found my niche. I thrived on helping people to grow their businesses on their terms (I still do), and the methods that I had unwittingly developed on my journey worked for others very successfully.

Over time, I realised that when executed properly, my methods worked for any business owner whose audience spent time on LinkedIn, and I expanded my client base to include business owners from lots of different industries. I offered 1:1 coaching, group coaching and corporate masterclasses in-house for businesses. Those who adopted my methods were very successful and happy to recommend me to all of their friends and colleagues, so I was never short of work.

However, the more people that I worked with, the more I realised that the success of my methods didn't just depend on strategy. They depended on the mindset to execute the strategy. Most of my clients had started a business because they are great at what they do. However, that didn't suddenly mean that they became confident to stand in the spotlight as the face of their business from Day 1.

Mindset and Marketing

Personal branding is an extremely successful method of marketing because it builds scalable know, like and trust with your audience. However, it hinges on you showing up with confidence as the face of your business, posting regular content and images and videos, and let's be honest, that can be a bloody scary thing to do- especially if you are not from a sales background.

I began to see that mindset and marketing were intrinsically linked. Patterns emerged amongst my clients. It wasn't that they didn't want to be visible as the face of their business. They desperately did. However, for some, in order to implement the strategy and become confident as the face of their business, they first had to overcome their visibility blocks. And whilst I could help them with the benefit of my own experience, I had no formal mindset training. Therefore, in April 2023, I made the huge decision to become qualified as a positive psychology coach so that I could impact my clients on a deeper level. This was a huge time commitment of 10 plus hours per week, but I knew in my heart that my business and my clients needed this, so I committed to an accelerated program, and I got stuck in.

As I trained in positive psychology, I began to research sales and visibility blocks and became more acquainted with the subconscious mind. I also realised that just as we as business owners have sales and visibility blocks- our potential clients often have buying blocks.

I came across an amazing coach called Gaby Abrams in the US who was pioneering something called Subconscious Marketing, which was a way of writing content that helped your prospects to overcome their own blocks to moving forward. It led to business owners being able to use subconscious marketing techniques to genuinely add value to their audience and attract the people that they would love to work with and have the most impact on. Gaby had an opportunity to train to teach subconscious marketing, and I saw this as the last missing piece of my business. So, even though I was already studying positive psychology, I embarked on Subconscious Marketing as an additional qualification, it just felt right.

By September 2023, I emerged as a qualified positive psychology coach who was also certified to teach Subconscious Marketing. Not only could I now help my clients to overcome their sales and visibility blocks, but I could teach them my strategies to build a successful personal brand on LinkedIn, AND help them to accelerate their results and impact by teaching them how to use subconscious marketing in their content.

I rebranded as a LinkedIn and Visibility Coach, and even though I had spent a lot of time studying, 2023 became my best year ever in my business. Why? Because I upleveled myself and started operating at a different level, and I gave my audience what they truly needed. I focused on having more impact, and as it always does, the money then followed.

Constantly evolving as a business owner and as a person is so important. So is always going back to your why for doing what you do (my family). Always follow your intuition. It's okay to change your mind or your direction or both. In the end, you will emerge as a stronger business owner and person. It's so important that you run your business rather than it running you!

I now continue to work with small business owners all over the world who want to stand out confidently as the face of their business and build their own brand on LinkedIn, combining mindset with messaging, branding and practical LinkedIn training.

Why LinkedIn? There are so many reasons why I still think even now, that LinkedIn is still the very best platform on which to grow your business. From being able to build a VERY specific audience of the right people to LinkedIn working in the background whilst you are busy doing other things. If you would like to know more about either my own journey or how you can leverage LinkedIn to grow your OWN business, I would love to hear from you.

You can find me on:
LinkedIn: https://www.linkedin.com/in/lyndseymeredith/
Facebook: https://www.facebook.com/lyndseymeredithonline
Instagram: https://www.instagram.com/lyndseymeredithonline/
Email: **lyndsey@meredithcs.co.uk**

Look out for my book "The Obvious Choice" and the accompanying podcast which will be released in Autumn 2024.

CHAPTER 3
Anna Anderson
High Performance Coach / Spiritual Mentor

The Bottle of Gin

I waved my 4-year-old son, Isaac, goodbye as he walked down the hill with his dad. My heart broke with the overwhelming pain of it all. I closed the door and sank to the ground. I didn't know how to carry on anymore. I was emotionally and physically exhausted. I hated saying goodbye to Isaac and spending weekends apart, I hated the whole situation; and most of all, I hated myself. I felt lost, confused and desperately alone. I had absolutely no sense of self-worth and I didn't know who I was.

THE RISE OF THE FEMALE ENTREPRENEUR

I had spent my entire life living in an external world; people pleasing, partying, and building my corporate career. I had been so busy ticking the external boxes that I had paid absolutely no attention to who I really was and, in that moment, as my life collapsed into rock bottom, I could no longer avoid the pain and the emptiness – I had to let myself fall into it. I had absolutely no idea how to get myself out of the misery of the situation.

It suddenly became painfully obvious that none of the things I had been doing were going to work any longer, but in that moment, there was only one solution I knew. I peeled myself from the ground and took myself to the kitchen. I took a large and unopened bottle of gin down from the shelf and proceeded to drink the bottle – neat. It was 10.30am.

I woke the next day feeling as bad as you can imagine but also with a deep and very clear knowing. This could no longer continue. Isaac deserved better; I deserved better. What and how to do anything about it was beyond me. I had a relatively good and well-paid corporate job in London – it was exhausting trying to work to the level I had prior to being a Mum, especially as a single parent with a 3 hour commute every day.

Isaac was about to start school, and I desperately wanted to be there to take him and pick him up, but that was not going to be possible with the job I was doing. I would only see him every other weekend and I would have to pay someone to do the very thing I wanted so desperately to do, whilst I was in London doing a job I no longer loved. I think this was probably the final straw, the thing that pushed me to realise I had to make a change. But what on earth could I do? I was solely responsible for paying my mortgage and supporting my child. Surely leaving a 'sensible' job was the worst decision of all as a single parent?

I pondered and worried, what would earn money and give me the time I needed? My head pounding from the gin, I sat up in bed, opened my laptop and googled 'jobs for Mums'. At the top of the search was the opportunity to buy a yoga franchise. It said it was a good way for Mums to work around their children. I was out of shape; I knew very little about yoga and I had never run my own business before but something inside me said…'this is for you'. I grabbed my phone and dialled the number. By the end of that day, on a whim and a hangover, I had bought a yoga franchise on a credit card.

A New Voice

That week I went into my office and told my business coach what I was planning to do. I distinctly remember her telling me that I should take my time making this decision and not to rush into anything; but I had already decided. I handed in my notice and took the plunge. It felt like such a crazy idea and everyone around me told me so, I could see the doubt written across their faces. Yet something inside of me was so calm. I just KNEW it would be ok. I had no idea how it would be, but I trusted this feeling; it didn't feel like I had any other option anyway.

I worked my notice and dedicated my life to training and learning. It is important to clarify here, I did not have many savings, it was a huge risk and I HAD to make it work. There was something inside me that kicked in – it was survival, I had to provide for my son, there was no option. I started to get up early, I practiced yoga every single day, I read all the teachings and books I could get my hands on, and I did my qualifications. I left my job in October 2013 and launched my new yoga business in January 2014.

I used my local community Facebook group to talk about my classes, I made posters and flyers, I walked the streets delivering them through people's doors, I went to local fayres and even had cupcakes made with my business name on them! I did everything I could to market my classes and fill them. At the beginning one of the classes had 10 people in it which felt like such a great achievement, whilst another only had two people and one of those spaces I had given away! But still, the voice was there – 'it will be OK…keep going'. So, I did, one day at a time. I kept going.

Whilst I was working on building my business, something else was happening within me. Because I was teaching yoga, I had to get good at it. So, I practiced every single day. I watched 100s of different teachers and I practiced and practiced and practiced. And something magical began to happen. I started to find a new feeling of peace that I had never experienced before. I felt calm, relaxed, and joyful. I started to want to eat well and nourish my body because I wanted to maintain this good feeling. I stopped drinking. My friendship circles started to change…as I changed within, things started to change without.

I found a new calm and kind voice within me. One that told me I was good enough; I was loveable and that I could trust it would be OK. I started to meditate, and I felt joy. I began to love what I was doing. I could see that it was not only helping me, but it was helping the people who came to my classes. I stopped fighting with how my life was and decided to accept my situation and instead enjoy the time I did have with Isaac. I started to make enough money for us to live and I was able to take my son to school and pick him up every day. Whilst I was working hard to build my business and there were definite feelings of fear, over-time it all started to feel easier as a feeling of peace grew within me.

Listen to The Heart

For the next few years, I taught yoga, and I became well known in my community for what I did. My classes thrived and I realised how much I loved helping people and creating spaces for them to come and find relaxation and peace. I also began to realise that one yoga class a week was not enough for them to really gain the healings that were possible for my students. I wanted to help people more deeply. I decided to train in many different healing and coaching modalities from NLP to Emotional Freedom Technique and Nutrition and Metaphysics to energy healings from the Mystery Schools in the lineage of King Solomon.

I sold my yoga business and stopped teaching yoga altogether so that I could focus on these new tools. What I didn't know when this journey all started is that we all have a blueprint of our lives encoded into our DNA. Free will is the ability we have to choose between our heads and hearts. If we keep ignoring the calling within us, we will continually be met by the same hurdles until we find the courage to take the leap to change. I began to coach people in helping them overcome their fears and the blocks that were preventing them from really loving themselves and living their lives in alignment to who they really are.

Society teaches us that if we follow this one path, happiness will be available. Do well at school, get a job, get married, have kids, build your career – you will be set. But I had done all those things, and I was miserable. What I was noticing as I grew personally was that I had my own set of tools and gifts that I could bring to the world, and I could build my life in alignment to the things I was good at. I didn't need to be like or copy anyone else – I could just be myself and that was enough.

I noticed the same in the people I was working with. As I taught them to love themselves, to overcome the negative ego in their heads and to learn to live from the voice in their hearts. As they peeled back the years of limiting beliefs, the feelings of lack and of not being good enough – they started to shine with happiness, and they discovered their own capabilities and brilliance. My clients were discovering who they really were and building their lives in alignment to that, and it was the most joyful thing to witness.

I became deeply passionate about teaching people that love is the answer. That they must do the work to love themselves first before anything else. That they had to find the courage to quit the negative thinking, to stop people pleasing, and to put boundaries in place. I wrote a book about my teachings that has now sold over 50,000 copies worldwide. I couldn't believe it.

My life had become something beyond what I could have ever imagined. I received emails every day from people saying thank you, that my teachings had helped them make life-changing shifts. I was making more money than I could have ever thought possible for me, ALL whilst being there for my son and taking him to school and picking him up every day. It was a dream come true.

Trust

Here I am today, 10 years on from that crazy decision and I could not be more grateful to that younger, frightened version of myself. I now know who I am. I know my purpose and I know my values. That younger version of me had no idea of these things. Because I have so much clarity, I am able to serve and help people on the same journey and there is nothing that brings me more joy than to see people fall in love with who they are and realise the brilliance they have to offer the world that is not like anyone else's.

What I love the most is that we are on the cusp of waking up to living with so much more conscious awareness and this is a reality for everyone. The Heart Math Institute and many other amazing scientific organizations are now proving what spirituality has taught us for 1000s of years. Energy is a very real thing; we create our realities through vibration. When we focus on loving ourselves, and we work to raise our vibration through practicing joyful living, meditation, gratitude, and appreciation; we raise the frequency of our energy field, and this enables us to create and build a life that is filled with joy and empowerment.

Yes, we absolutely will face challenges in our lives – we are supposed to! They are there to build resilience and strength so that we are prepared to receive the next level of growth available to us. We are not victims to our situation as I once believed, our hearts have an incredible intelligence, far beyond the limited and fear-based thinking of the mind.

Your mind is designed to move away from pain. That means it's focused on all that has gone wrong in the past and all that could go wrong in the future. It remembers the time you felt embarrassed at school or when children were mean to you in the playground. It is programmed by the things your parents modelled for you and what society has said you should do, be and have. Living solely from the mind creates a life of fear, anxiety, shame, and limitation and sadly, it is where I see many people living their life experience from. It means they never really discover all the possibility that is available to them.

Your heart is designed to move towards joy. It will lead you towards the things that are meant for you, it will guide you towards your purpose. It will whisper ideas or thoughts to you – if you take the time to slow down and hear them. It takes great courage to step outside of the fear of your mind and to start to take steps towards the joy of your heart. To begin with, it might feel like you have less clarity about where you are going and that your path is not safe but ultimately what is required is trust.

By learning to live with trust that everything is working out for you, that your heart knows the way and that you can take one step at a time towards building the life of your dreams through saying yes to following your joy, your life will start to unfold in the most magical ways.

Your Encoded Magic

From one woman in business, to you, a woman who is either in business already or is thinking about taking that leap; here is my message to you…

YOU ARE AMAZING, BRILLIANT, CAPABLE AND FULL OF UNLIMITED POTENTIAL AND MAGIC. YOU HAVE GOT WHAT IT TAKES. KNOW THAT.

You have your own personal map of evolution encoded into your being. If you have a nagging feeling that there is something else or more out there for you, that is because there is!! If you have dreams of a different life, it is because those dreams are meant for you to realise. If you don't feel like you know your purpose at all, it doesn't matter – you one million per cent have one. It will become clear to you as you take the steps to love yourself instead of living in fear.

So, wherever you are on your journey, know this:

Love is the pathway to your joy. The first step you must take before you do anything else is to love yourself wholly and completely. You must let go of the limiting beliefs and QUIT being unkind to yourself. Stop saying yes when you want to say no. Stop pleasing others and thinking that you are not enough – YOU ARE. Do the work you need to do to release these patterns. Go to therapy, get a coach, connect with nature, breathe, meditate, and stop repeating the patterns that are no longer serving you. It is time for you to connect with your heart and speak your truth. The world needs healed and brave women. The world needs you in your authenticity and glory.

Understand energy. You are here to create your reality and you are manifesting all the time. We live in a vibrational reality. You are creating with your words, your thoughts, and your actions. Imagine the life you see before you is a mirror reflection of the image you hold within yourself. As you do the work to love yourself and clear up the limiting beliefs, you will start to see your external world shifting. You are not a victim; you are not stuck. You have very real capability, and you must stop speaking negatively because it energetically creates more of the same. Understand that what you focus upon, grows – so focus on what is good.

Fear is designed to keep you small and stuck in your comfort zone. It will tell you all sorts of stories about how rubbish you are, how fat you look and how much you have failed in the past. ALL OF THAT IS RUBBISH. If you listen to the limitations of fear in your mind, your life will become smaller and smaller and more and more stressful. Your true and authentic life can ONLY EXIST outside of your comfort zone so you must learn to dance with fear and take steps outside of your comfort every single day. As you grow, the next thing will be new so it will be scary – that does not mean you should not do it, it means you should! Often, the scariest thing is the thing that is meant for us. Do the thing!

Gratitude is one of the most powerful tools you have. It can shift your vibration with immediate effect. Take the time to slow down and notice what is already good in your life. Remember, what you focus upon, you create more of. We have been taught by society to be happy when we have the evidence, but you must flip your thinking and realise that to be happy, you need to do the work to create joy within yourself first. Gratitude is a master key at enabling you to shift your experience and create a life filled with all you desire. What you feel now, you are creating more of – so do what it takes to be joyful NOW, not when you reach your next goal.

Action is a necessity. New age thinking often says we can manifest our dreams by thinking positively and whilst thinking positively will certainly help, you need to do more. You must act towards your goals. Stop hoping, wishing, and talking about what you want or need to do and DO IT. To manifest, it starts with an idea – a spark of intuition. Next comes the thinking about the idea, followed by the planning and then comes the action. It is normal for people to get stuck in one or more of these areas but to create your dream reality, you must do them all. Have the courage to act. Do the thing that scares you.

You are here to learn and grow. You have never failed; you have simply learned through your experiences. Life does not need to be so serious; it is supposed to be fun and full of joy.

You get one time here – make the most of it, live it to the edges of your capacity. Laugh more often, say yes to things that scare you and please – most of all, learn to love the bones of your being. Because my love, you are magnificent, and your life is your work of art. Go and create it as if no one was watching and then stand back and bask in the glory of the beautiful vision that you have created. Build your empire, one day at a time. Your dreams are totally possible for you.

Anna Anderson

www.annaa.com

CHAPTER 4
Karen Deulofeu
Lily Ama Coaching
Fertility, Pregnancy & Postnatal Coach

It all began without an egg

It was the best year of my life. A year in Spain as part of my university course. I'd never have guessed how it would unfold.

It was an odd requirement, before we left the UK, to have a medical check-up. Fit and healthy, I did it and took the chance to ask about an odd lump on my tummy. I was cautious not to be paranoid, but it was worth a mention. The

GPs professional opinion was I just needed a poo, so nothing to worry about(!), or so we thought. How wrong she was... we all make mistakes, right?

Off I went to Spain and had the time of my life. Understanding very little at first, I threw myself into the language, culture, and food. I was placed in the Universidad de Sevilla studying Law to match my UK studies. A law degree was difficult enough in England, in Spain it was bonkers! I'd sit in the lecture hall surrounded by keen students diligently writing notes. With my limited understanding of the complex Spanish legal terminologies, and therefore lectures, I spent the time writing letters home. At least this way it looked like I was taking notes and listening!

At Christmas, my two-week visit back home led to 2 months in bed that changed everything.

I'd joke to my then boyfriend about my "Spanish belly". My tummy was visibly rounder than it had been, and I put it down to a change in diet and lifestyle. I didn't think anything of it and was eager to get back to Spain. I had two months left in Seville before moving on to Barcelona to put my learning into practice working in a law firm.

After his persistent concerns and cajoling, I saw the GP the day before I was due to fly back to Spain, fully expecting it to be nothing, and be told to have a poo again! As it turns out, I didn't return until three months later.

The fake pregnancy

Lying on the couch, the GP (the same one who told me to have a poo five months previously) proudly announced I was six months pregnant having found a heartbeat. I knew for sure that was impossible, and she reluctantly checked my wrist and confirmed it was my heartbeat. This happened three times! After doing a negative pregnancy test, the next step was a scan.

The scan revealed a massive cyst. The doctors anticipated surgery, indicating an extended recovery period. The seriousness escalated further in subsequent consultant appointments. In one I was told the recovery time of surgery would be like that of a hysterectomy – 6 weeks of barely lifting and lots of rest. A move back to Spain seemed a long way away.

Realising the seriousness, we decided to undergo surgery near home in Cornwall where family could support. In the final appointment, expecting a date to be set for surgery in the coming weeks, I was urged to go home, pack a bag and come right back. Surgery would be that night. There was a risk, given the size of the cyst, akin to a watermelon by now, that it could burst at any time, and if it did, I'd not be here to tell this story.

Pre surgery, something happened that created a big shift in my mind, and ultimately my career.

The surgeon kindly explained the surgery might require all my reproductive organs to be removed, my womb and both ovaries. I refused. I knew there and then I didn't want my chances of having children taken away. That if this was my time, it was my time.

They could take the ovary and cyst, but nothing else. I went into surgery not quite knowing what would happen or what they'd find, but believing I'd had a pretty good run at this thing we call life.

It was such a rollercoaster. Had the GP taken the lump seriously at the beginning, I'd likely just have needed tablets or a laparoscopy, just minor surgery. Suddenly, it was major surgery that could have so easily been avoided.

The relief turned confusion

As it turns out, an ovary was removed and a biopsy from the other was taken. The cyst was the size of a melon, a baby. After 2 hours of surgery, I dropped more than a dress size and lots of weight. The best diet, but not something I'd wish on anyone.

From that point, I became focused on when I should start a family. With one ovary left, the surgeon advised I'd need to be trying to conceive by 27; otherwise, it might be too late. By this point I was due to go back to Spain, mid-way through university and in no position mentally, financially, or practically to have a baby.

Recovery was hard, and my return to Spain was tricky. I was still sore and feeling bewildered at everything that had happened. I went back a different person.

As time went on, 27 passed, as did that relationship and my life, choices and actions took a different turn. Almost like a delayed rebellion, outwardly I was the happy-go-lucky one. Inside, I was foggy and scared.

In hindsight and to others, these thoughts were unnecessary and overdramatic. However, having fallen down the hole it was hard to see the light again. With a scar from my belly button down I was visibly damaged, felt broken and less of a woman, half of what I needed to be a mum.

I'd repeatedly ask doctors when I needed to conceive by, looking for reassurance, but the response was always bleak.

Put on the contraceptive pill to conserve what eggs I had left wasn't the ideal reason, and it repeated my worries. Early days with a new guy I'd try to gauge if/when this could be the one, without asking the inevitable question. It was a confusing rollercoaster of living a carefree life while wanting to settle down.

Internal scarring was painful, and a laparoscopy to address it led to 2 months of constant bleeding. When the pain returned, I refused more surgery to preserve what I had left and lived with regular pain for years.

It was a dark time, and as the years went on, it was feeling more and more bleak. With the seed sown that 27 would be my last chance, as I flew past 27, a fear for the future set in. I'd question my purpose, goals and future. Not wanting to be here because I didn't feel secure in my own skin. Self-belief had been lost; I barely knew myself anymore. So often ladies trying to conceive, or experiencing loss, feel like this. It's hard to understand and even harder to explain.

The theatre

I saw counsellors with limited success. We talked about the past, resulting only in sections of my life being painfully and unnecessarily blocked out but never really healed. I was swimming in mud and didn't have the tools to get out.

As many do, throwing myself into work seemed like a good option. I became a lawyer and later moved into insurance with an enviable job requiring regular travel to South America investigating insurance claims. With my successful role, it was suggested I chose work over family. Nothing could be further from the truth. It was a cover. Something to hold onto if I couldn't be a mum, but it was more like uncomfortable theatre.

Everything came to a head in Mexico... on a normal day, I crashed. It all came tumbling out of me. How, in my early 20s, over four years, I'd experienced the fragility of life: my brother was hit by a car in front of my eyes, supporting mum through breast cancer and chemo, my emergency surgery. It was too much, and at that point, I didn't know where to turn and even questioned if I wanted to be here anymore at all.

It all started to work out

Soon after that things started to turn around. At age 35, I met the man I'd later marry. Things moved fast and we were on the same page with children and aspirations. A year later we were married. We bought and renovated a home. We began trying for a baby.

After years of believing I may not be able to conceive when the baby didn't come, we went to the GP hoping to be given pills and reassurance. Instead, we were sent to a specialist, and it all started moving quickly.

Because of my age and having only one ovary, we were encouraged to start IVF quickly. I should have been happy but instead was devastated. Something that should be natural, felt scientific and final. I was terrified of what it would mean if this didn't work, where'd we go from there?

Right before IVF, at a fun birthday party, I looked around and felt lost again. Surrounded by women with children, I felt less feminine, alone, bewildered. I didn't know who I was or represented anymore. It seemed at every corner someone was pregnant or pushing a pram.

The IVF saga

Right before we started treatment a scan showed my other tube was badly damaged and had to be removed. More devastation and intense guilt that this was due to my "delayed rebellion". With one ovary and no tubes, IVF was the only way forward.

For the first IVF, I did what we're all told – was positive. I imagined the baby (a girl) gave her a name (Liliana) and visualised playing with her (on the bed cooing). I told myself IVF was needed simply to connect the dots, and this would be our time.

When it didn't work, I hit a new low. I'd been so positive it felt so real and a heavy loss. Even though only a failed cycle so many hopes had been pinned on it. This is why I always say every cycle, every loss at any stage is significant. They were all the chance, a potential. Let's stop dismissing the losses pre-12 weeks.

I was hit with the realisation that no matter how positive I was, it was fake. The years of thinking it wouldn't happen, and preparing myself for the worst, had taken their toll. It left me distrusting of my body's ability to get and stay pregnant. With the added story of my mum's pregnancy struggles and late loss, there was little wonder. My body and mind were disconnected – positive without the necessary belief.

By addressing the distrust through coaching and EFT (Emotional Freedom Technique), I finally started to rebuild my self-belief and inner trust. I stopped fighting against my thoughts. I learnt how to cope better and went into the next IVF feeling more grounded, less frazzled, and more on an even keel. More hopeful without the anxiety. That time, it worked!

Pregnancy after IVF – the reality

Finally, I was pregnant, the thing I'd always wanted, so why couldn't I just relax into it and enjoy it like I'd imagined?

The years of preparing myself for never being a Mum had taken their toll. Even though I was pregnant, the worry it would end was never far away. Even though there were no medical concerns, I found myself living scan to scan, as many do who've experienced loss or infertility before pregnancy. My midwife was incredible, a true support, but didn't know what to suggest.

We're all encouraged to talk about how we're feeling and to be more aware of our mental health. However, there's another step that's often missed – knowing what to do with it. It's one thing to put your hand up and say you're struggling, but knowing how to move on is key. I was firmly in the spot of not knowing.

Desperate to enjoy pregnancy, I was saving receipts just in case I didn't bring him home. It was a true rollercoaster throughout. After a traumatic birth, 15 years of believing I wouldn't be a mum and IVF, finally holding my son in my arms was a blessing I barely dared I'd experience. My parenting style was dictated by my journey and, at times felt at odds with my personality. We were both as needy as each other of physical touch and reassurance yet desperate for alone time.

As a family, it was apparent some practical and emotional support would have been invaluable in the early days. Counsellors were lovely, but I didn't need to spend time talking about what had happened. We needed something more proactive. To know how to better manage the huge spikes of emotions that come with parenting whilst maintaining our cool and deepening our relationships. We didn't get the support we needed; we were coming apart at the seams.

A bumpy ride

As a new couple with a baby, navigating it all is mind-boggling. We could have handled it better but didn't know how. We'd not been taught and were lost in the sleepless nights and baby fog.

A couple of weeks after our son turned one, his dad announced he was leaving. It had gotten too much, and unable to see past the fog, he'd made his decision. I was terrified of being alone with a 1-year-old and holding down a busy corporate job – by then Head of Client Success across EMEA for a large legal tech firm. As it turns out, we went into Covid lockdown a month later, so working from home somewhat helped the transition, but it was still huge.

Feeling frustrated and angry that there had to be a better way to navigate fertility, pregnancy, and new parenting started the best chapter in my life! Something had to be learnt from my 15-year rollercoaster. No one else should suffer the same way I had, or families break down as a result.

The legacy of infertility/loss had to be broken. There had to be a better way. Training courses to become a fertility coach spiked my interest. The more I learnt the more I realised this is the gap that needed filling.

It's not about the baby – it's about us and how we live the journey. How in control we feel. How much of life gets lost to fears. How much time is paused waiting for appointments. How we lose ourselves in the process. How our identity shifts and morphs. How our spark goes. The impact this has on our work, our focus, our relationships, social connections, and family. We deserve to know how to change the narrative and live life on our terms while going through this.

It's not only about the baby, it's about us – It must start with us, but how?

Giving back, a new way

My experience, good, bad, and ugly, fuelled a passion and determination to learn a different way. With a glimmer of how that looked, I felt the need to teach others. To not only offer support but also teach a different method. One that gave back emotional control, stability, security, and a sense of empowerment that's otherwise lost along the way.

As I trained, suddenly it all became clear. People noticed the shift in me. My mum mentioned that the day of the surgery some 15 years ago, the spark went... and it had returned. Doesn't everyone deserve to not live those years in the dark? This had to be shared!

My training began as a Fertility Support Specialist. A year of learning various techniques within a designated program to support emotional well-being through infertility and loss. A blend of counselling, coaching, and mind/body techniques, it gave clients the peace they were looking for and the tools to trust themselves more and to feel more in control of their journey, rather than be controlled by it. Delivering the program, the positive results were evident session by session.

Not wanting to end at fertility, having experienced how pregnancy is affected by the journey there, I also trained as a Pregnancy and Postnatal Support Specialist. Similarly, this was a program I delivered to support clients' emotional well-being at this crucial time.

These programs and resources gave me an understanding and invaluable insight into my client's needs, my own and the wonderful world of coaching.

Back to school

With knowledge and even more drive, I saw ways to develop my own program, add new tools, and grow further. As an ex-lawyer, I knew training first was imperative. So, I took to the books and classroom again!

At the time, still in corporate, with existing clients, a single mama to a rambunctious 2-year-old, I embarked on in-depth training to become an NLP, EFT and Hypnosis Practitioner, as well as a Life & Success Coach and Mindset Transformation Coach. With these tools in my pocket, Lily Ama Coaching was truly born – my 2nd baby!

Bespoke programs were developed, 1 for each of Fertility, Pregnancy & Postnatal. A mini taster program, written and audio resources were created to further support my clients' journeys.

My practice is focused on working through subconscious blocks to change the narrative for good. To heal the hurt, live the present and look to the future differently. Learn tools to support our mental and emotional well-being day in/day out whatever comes our way. To ditch the fake positivity and replace it with true self-belief and trust.

Since leaving corporate, I've supported people through infertility, childlessness, loss (miscarriage and stillbirth), birth trauma, secondary infertility, donor conception, female and male factor infertility and more. My clients range from same-sex couples, single mamas and heterosexual couples—a beautiful range of incredible, inspirational individuals.

I pride myself on having built a network of specialists who I regularly refer people to if they're looking for a different type of support too.

For the fertility work, I wondered that people would come to me with the sole aim of getting pregnant. I couldn't have been more wrong. They want to cope better, manage the rollercoaster, drop their anxiety. It's about moving on from the trauma of the journey, the frustration, the regret and the hurt. To feel feminine again, to refocus at work, rekindle relationships, enjoy life instead of putting it on hold. To stop living cycle to cycle. The impact of achieving this is huge.

In pregnancy, it's more often about enjoyment instead of living scan to scan. Not holding on to receipts just in case. It's about looking forward to the scans without trepidation because it's another chance to see their baby. Healing from the hurt of previous experiences and daring to believe this is your time. Building memories that will last forever and will be retold with joy.

Postnatally, it's about finding yourself again amidst the chaos of new parenthood. Keeping a strong relationship. Bonding in a way that's right for you and your family. Growing in this new chapter without falling apart. Enjoying it.

Overall, it's about rebuilding self-belief and trust in our minds and bodies. For this reason, my practice isn't focused on the baby. It's on the person. Whatever is coming up while on this journey. This way the things we learn are transferable to other areas and so much more meaningful. It's learning a new way to navigate all of life while on this journey with someone who's been there and gets it.

A toolbox

When my son started school, parents were invited to create a physical box of resources for the children when they're feeling anxious to help regulate their feelings. It got me thinking… how many of us have a "toolbox" of resources that we know can help us when we're struggling. Having a day off, going for a massage is all well and good – but what happens when we have that difficult conversation at work the next day? We all deserve to know the tools to help us manage the difficult times.

Within my practice, I give people the tools to build their toolbox, and the results are incredible. They feel less stressed, more in control, able to cope, whole and most of all, they reach their big goals. We share all moments. I'm here to hold their hand, cheer them on at the side-lines, and celebrate the wins every step of the way. I genuinely couldn't be happier.

The trouble with being positive

There's a difference between positivity and self-belief. We can all fake positivity, but many lack the tools to build and maintain real self-belief. Most of us are trying to see in the dark. We want to follow a map, but the GPS is off. And we've no idea where the on button is.

How would it be if there was a different story? My focus is on fertility, pregnancy and postnatal because that's where it all starts. That's where so many of us need the support.

I teach clients to understand themselves better. To be more in control of their emotions instead of being controlled by them. To have tools they can go to time and time again when the going gets tough. Even more, tools that can easily fit into their lives, so things don't get so tough again.

We fix the cause, not the problem. Often there's a pattern of behaviour that's led to a belief that dictates our actions. We work through all of this proactively. Most of our actions are controlled by our subconscious mind, only 5% by our conscious mind. If we spend all our time thinking, we spin. By making a change at a subconscious level, the impact is wide-ranging and long-lasting. It becomes a way of life and a way that feels better day in day out. We feel more secure and confident as a result.

Once we feel positive at the core, we never have to think ourselves positive again. Once we understand ourselves, we can seamlessly go to the root cause and address it, without going through the pain.

My coaching is typically delivered in 1:1 programs, group courses and corporate workshops. Each one provides a tried and tested, science-backed framework alongside a personalised approach. The method is based on being proactive, future-paced with present healing.

Alleviating the need to remember everything I teach, guides are given highlighting the why and how of everything we go through together. Session overviews are provided to capture the key areas we talked about in each personalised session. Best of all, you get a "coach in your pocket" direct access to me via voice/text message anytime you need it between sessions. Knowing there's someone to support you as things arise, and offer tools, and reminders of what you've learnt is the magic. It's a nudge to remind you – you've got this. It embeds all the learnings even deeper.

I offer a unique perspective as someone who's gone through this while holding down a corporate job, playing the theatre of being ok and crumbling inside. I know how it feels and can uniquely support others, so they get the best out of the program and, more importantly, themselves.

My practice has been so successful I also support others in becoming coaches themselves. Guiding them in building a business of their very own. I offer corporate workshops to give more understanding and space to talk in a business environment.

My drive is simple – no one should experience what I did. We all deserve to know about the tools we have available inside of us but have not yet been taught how to use them. We deserve to heal without the trauma of reliving in minute detail.

Most of all – we deserve to live in a world where we do not feel alone, where infertility isn't stigmatised. Where the next generation of women won't feel broken or unfeminine if it takes them longer to conceive, or they don't have children. We deserve to heal and enjoy our pregnancies and postnatal journeys in a way that's right for us.

THE RISE OF THE FEMALE ENTREPRENEUR

I want to live in a world where people going through this feel heard, supported and unafraid. How about you?

Book a free call: https://calendly.com/lily_ama/30-min-discovery-call

Website: www.lilyamacoaching.co.uk
Instagram: https://www.instagram.com/fertilitycoach.lilyama/
LinkedIn: https://www.linkedin.com/in/karendeulofeu/

CHAPTER 5
Andrea Rainsford
Women Winning in Business

"You'll Never Walk Alone Again"

My favourite pastime as a child was dashing into my parents off-licence in Birmingham and sinking my teeth into a bar of Cadburys chocolate before they could take it off me. Well, they couldn't sell it with my teeth marks on it, could they? That gives a clear idea of the type of child I was. Enterprising! I was a cheeky, mischievous, and noisy child. I could always be heard, if not be seen.

My Nan was my person, we were a little team. My parents worked full time, so my Nan took care of me from morning till night. My dad had a full-time job and also worked in the off-licence in the evening. My parents worked hard; I believe I gained my work ethic from watching them.

Nan taught me so much, her values, her sayings, and her proverbs, all stay with me to this day. I remember her taking me to my first day at school, holding my hand, smiling at me and telling me, "I'll be back at lunchtime, I know you will make so many friends." It was true, I did make many friends that day, splashing around in the water playpens, building sandcastles, I had the best time. I learnt to be independent from an exceedingly early age. Nan taught me how to cook. We cooked Dad steamed suet puddings, jam tarts, stews, and roast dinners. She taught me how to sew, but most of all, she taught me independence and how to rely on myself.

Our family consisted of Mom, Dad, big brother Simon, Nan, Grandad, and me. We also had Tara the Alsatian dog, Tibby the Cat, and George the Budgie! My brother was the intelligent one, with an exceptional memory. At four years old, he could stock the off-license shelves by matching the label shapes and colours. He would sit with my Grandad at the kitchen table doing sum after sum effortlessly. Me? I always had somewhere to be, something to do, someone to see. I never sat still and never shut up either. He could often be heard saying, "Can't you take her somewhere for an hour?" my noise levels were a little on the loud side.

Grandad left us when I was around eight, and Nan and I were always together, just the two of us. Simon was older and always out with his friends. She walked me to and from school each day and always had the biscuit tin open and a warm drink when I returned home in the evenings. Sadly, she left me when I was 13. My world stopped. Time seemed to stand still. Mom and Dad were working full-time, and Simon was at college. It was a time when I felt so alone in the world. My rock, my person, my constant, was gone.

The years after she left were some of the toughest. Mom was Mom, she was not the most patient person, she worked hard and became tired and irritable easily. She started to drink a lot after Nan left and did not take her passing well. I was now in charge. At 13 I did the housework, and the cooking and had everything ready for when they all came home. The loneliness from not being seen, not being heard, and not having a person made me withdraw.

The noisy, cheeky girl was gone.

It was around this time that the feelings of inadequacy started. I was invisible. Everyone in the family had busy lives and I simply did not fit. I was not able to attend after-school clubs, I needed to be home to walk the dog, do the chores, and cook the tea. It was simply the way it was. The monitoring of my weight, the monitoring of what I ate, and over-exercising started here. I decided I simply was not good enough. My GCSE grades were average. I was average.

I failed my A levels due to a boy, my first ever boy. I was simply besotted with him and all the attention. Someone could see me, actually see me. Someone wanted me. The failure of the A levels meant the need to work; uni was not now not an option. I'd had a business degree place at Derby Uni; however, it was a dream I would never realise. Or would I?

At the tender age of 18, I started my corporate career, and business development was to be my trade of choice. I cut my teeth with GVA Grimley at Brindley Place, Birmingham. I had the time of my life at corporate events, awards ceremonies, and lavish networking events, nothing I had ever seen or experienced before. I was loving this new life, I was loving the attention, I was loving that for the first time, I was great at something.

Things Were Going So Well

Being good at something is infectious, isn't it? It can become a drug, the serotonin you feel from the praise, the adulation. So, addictive. Addicted I was. Work became my life, my whole life. Well, there was a little bit of time to kill myself in the gym! When I was not making myself sick from bulimia, I was killing myself on a cardio machine of some description.

Looking back, it is a miracle my body held out as long as it did. I am quite proud of it for holding on. I think resilience was always in me, always there. I simply could not see it. So, I moved from GVA Grimley to Ernst & Young, where I worked in the 'sexy' division of Corporate Finance. I managed their pipeline, their key accounts, their pitches, and their business development. I spent many happy hours at networking events with Lloyds Development Capital, 3i, Springboard, and Royal Bank of Scotland. It was the norm, and I was brilliant at bringing people together, creating dynamic partnerships and getting deals done. It is a wonder my liver survived, being in corporate you need to constantly build your network and as this sector was male-dominated, the networking was done with a glass or a golf club in your hand.

Things were going so well that I bought my first home, alone, just me, on my own. How proud was I!

Then I met the man of my dreams; he helped me move into my new home, and well, he never went home. It looked like he was staying for good! At the age of 29, I was headhunted by Eversheds to head up their Business

Development team for the Employment Law Division. A complete change, but Business Development is all the same. I had my team to manage, and in the short time I was there, we were on fire. In 8 short months, I landed Renault, Peugeot, 3i, BBC and BAA as clients.

Life had never felt better—however, later that year. I never worked again.

My body had taken all it could. I collapsed in the middle of a pitch meeting, and that was the last time I worked; it was my last day in a corporate office. I had private healthcare and the doctors spent months trying to diagnose me. The consultant said to me, 'You'll never work again." You may think this is the title of this chapter, but not quite. The title refers to another conversation, which I will share with you shortly.

I was diagnosed with M.E. in 2003, my body had burnt out. I had pushed and pushed, exercise, lack of food, 80-hour weeks. Pushing to be seen, to be loved, to be wanted, to be anything other than who I was. In true Andrea style, I was not going to take this lying down, and I fought back.

Ian, the man of my dreams loved me for me which was a strange and funny feeling. He will tell you that I did everything in my power to put him off and make him leave. How could he possibly want to be with me? We became a family of 3 shortly after we met. Ebby, the black tiny 1-year-old dumped rescue cat, made us complete—a little family.

We went on to get married in 2004. It was a tough day, my body wanted to sleep and rest all the time, I had after all broken it. I struggled to stand and walk, but we did have the best Wedding Day! He loved me, and he married me even though I was sick. He must be something special, mustn't he?

I am sad to say that in September 2005, he came home and found me unconscious, and that day changed everything. I had properly done it this time; I had really broken me. I'd had a stroke. Not a little one, not a small one, not a tiny one. One that took my left side. I could not walk, feed, dress, wash, or toilet myself. S*hit.

We have dreams, ideals, and plans of how we think life will be. Of how we think life will pan out, don't we? The picture in your mind's eye of what your wedding dress will look like, of meeting your dream man, the family home, life with children running around the garden, growing old together. My dreams all disappeared in an instant.

I lay in my small bed in a large cold hospital, feeling all alone in the world. The reality was I was not alone. I was surrounded by five older ladies, all with dementia, strokes, and broken limbs, all needing care and rehab to help them return home one day soon. We all had one thing in common, we could not walk, wash, or go to the toilet alone.

I have been asked many times how I felt at this time, how I got through the days, and how I did not despair and give up on life. The truth is I did not know how long I was going to be in there. I did not know how long it was going to take me to recover. But I always had one thing...

Hope

Hope got me through each day. Maybe today is the day they will let me go home, today will be the day I will walk again. I spent six months altogether in hospital, getting to know the nurses by their first names, the doctors popping in for a coffee when they were passing. I was 32, and you could tell they felt sorry for me. The pitying looks, the holding of my hand, the extra hot chocolate in the middle of the night when I could not sleep. They all made my time bearable.

Old habits reared their head. The lack of control led to me trying to take back any form of control in any way. I started to control my eating. It was the only option available to me. I stopped eating, and I told myself it was okay. It would all be okay if I was just slimmer and lost a few pounds. I thought the nurses were so busy, that they would not notice what I was eating, or what I was consuming, because they had so many of us to look after. But notice they did. The nutritionist arrived and explained they were going to insert a feeding tube. This had gotten serious.

I promised to behave, I promised I would eat again if she helped me with my weight control and did not allow me to pile on the pounds whilst I was in bed and unable to do any form of exercise, and she agreed. We made a pact and as I had a special diet, special foods, just for me, I started to eat again.

The days and weeks passed. I remember looking out of the window and seeing all the Christmas decorations in the streets, everyone Christmas shopping and being together with their families. I had many lonely days. I was in hospital for so long, and it was impossible to have visitors every day. Ian tried his best, as did my beautiful dad, but it was so tiring on them, they needed rest too. I will never be able to thank them enough for their love and care during this time, it will stay with me until the day I die.

It was around Christmas time when one of the Doctors said to me, "You'll never walk again." Ian looked at me, and I looked at him. I said to Ian, "He doesn't know me, does he?" And that is when the fight started. Right then, that minute. I went to rehab where I had my own room overlooking beautiful gardens in the countryside. I missed my ladies; I did however have a lady with a Zimmer who used to stop by and chat when she was doing her laps of the corridor. I so looked forward to her coming, clicking down the hall. I always knew she would stop by and take the time of day.

I spent Christmas Day in the rehab facility, and they were amazing. I was still bedbound, but they laid a table for Ian with crackers and a Christmas tablecloth. They served him a 2-course lunch with a tipple from the drinks trolley. I can remember us fondly sitting there together, acting as if everything was completely normal. It felt it, on that day at least.

Home is Where the Heart Is

In February 2006, they allowed me home. They had tried everything to get me walking and toileting myself to no avail. It was time for me to go home. Home to Ian and Ebby. I have no words to describe how much I had missed Ebby, she was my furry child. I had been away from her for over six months. I can remember the journey home in the ambulance wondering if she would remember me, wondering if she would still love me. They kept me flat all the way home and I so longed to see the world again and look out of the windows.

The ambulance came to a halt, and they took me to the front room of my home, where a hospital bed was waiting for me in our living room. Ian had to sell our furniture to get it in. The stark reality of the journey ahead came into view. The ambulance men hoisted me into bed and settled me in. I lay there taking in my new surroundings, I had not been here for such a long time. Then I heard the patter of tiny paws on the stairs, and in she came, tail in the air and jumped up on the bed, and there she stayed. Right by my side.

The first team of carers arrived at 6 pm that evening, two young teenage girls. They came in chatting, pulled down the bedclothes, pulled down my underwear, rolled me over, and did not say one word to me, not one word. I lay in the dark and sobbed and sobbed, how did I get here?

Ian and Ebby then became my security team. Ian vetted all the carers from this point on. Most of the agency team were scared to come to our house as Ian would be watching and woe be tied to them if they did not take amazing care of me. Ebby would be in situ and would be incredibly difficult to move, offering a growl to all who came near, she had her eye on them.

We gained a routine. The carers became friends, we found our rhythm, and as mortifying as it is to have a stranger wash you, change you, and toilet you, you simply do not have a choice, and it could not all be left to Ian.

I had a team. A team to bring me back to life, a team to help me find my way, a social worker, a physio, an OT, carers, Ian, friends, and family and of course, Ebby. We all planned to get me back to health. I told them I WOULD walk again. I am not sure they believed me. I told them I would achieve it, I could see it, I could feel it, I could breathe it.

I would love to tell you it happened quickly. It did not. I would love to tell you that the following year I bounced back, and all was fine and dandy. It was not. I always had hope and I always had determination.
There were days I gave up, so many of them.

Days where I would cry, have tantrums, cry myself to sleep, and refuse to see people. Days where I would hate myself and my body. Days where I could not see a future. I did not leave the house for many years; in total, I spent seven years in that hospital bed. I did start to go out for short periods of time after 2-3 years. The odd trip to the shops and the odd concert, where we would get amazing seats. There had to be some rewards of being in a wheelchair! Life was starting to return.

Not quick enough for me. I am sure by now you have worked out, I am not known for my patience; I am not known for letting the grass grow under my feet. So, in 2009 I decided that I was going to go back to university. When I told Ian he walked out of the room!

He was nervous, he was scared, he wanted to wrap me in cotton wool and take care of me. I needed to know if my brain still worked. Was I still me? Could I still be me? You may remember I said earlier in the chapter that my dream of a degree and going to uni was gone, or was it? Well. I was damn well going to give it a good try. So of I went in my wheelchair with my carers. Try I did, and in 2013, the week of my 40th birthday, I graduated with a degree in Computing Science. I walked with crutches into my Graduation ceremony. The cheer that went up was deafening. I will never ever forget it. Dream one: tick!

So, what next?

The thing was, I would not be going to work anytime soon. I had my degree, it had been so hard, harder than I ever thought possible. The tiredness, the tests, the exams and with such a poor memory and a body that was not used to doing anything at all, I was struggling. I wanted and needed to contribute to the household again. I had been the main earner when we met. I bought our homes, and Ian did not mind in the slightest, he loved that I loved my job and that I loved providing for us. It was time for me to contribute again.

Business One: SEO Angel was born in 2014. She is ten years old this year, 2024. The pride is immense. Looking back on writing this chapter in this book has made me realise what I have achieved and what I have overcome.

Never EVER doubt what you are capable of, NEVER!

Last year, in 2023, 10 years after walking into my graduation ceremony. I finally WALKED again WITHOUT AID. 18 years after the stroke, I walked, unaided, on my own, with my own two feet! I am crying while writing this. I was determined it would happen. However, I was not sure deep down it would ever happen. But happen it did, and I now walk around freely. I am not sure I will ever lose the excitement of walking down the road on my own in my walking boots and playing around in the mud.

Business Two: Andrea Rainsford Creating Business Growth was born in 2023. Time to get back to my roots, time to get back to what I was brilliant at, time to step into her shoes once again.

So, thank you for reading.

My parting words of my chapter to you:

You are amazing, you are fabulous, never ever doubt what is possible and what you can achieve!

The world is yours for the taking.

Andrea xx

Call to Action: https://linktr.ee/andrearainsford

Andrea Rainsford – Women Winning in Business

THE RISE OF THE FEMALE ENTREPRENEUR

CHAPTER 6
Dorothy Norris
The Reluctant, Sceptical Network Marketer

Catalyst

'No problem,' he said. 'All you have to do is keep going as you are, and you'll be able to retire at 85.'

'Do you know anyone who wants an 85-year-old midwife?' I asked.

I don't think he had thought about what he was saying. The words simply popped out of his mouth, but they left me with dread in the pit of my stomach. That worry knot grew tighter and tighter over the next few weeks. I couldn't sleep. I began to dread the on-calls.

THE RISE OF THE FEMALE ENTREPRENEUR

The background to all of this is that I was the sole income earner for our family of 4, with a mortgage and two teenagers to put through university. I would just have to grit my teeth and keep working. But I knew that wasn't the answer. There must be a way out. I couldn't keep going at the pace I'd set myself over the past few years. I was working both as an Independent Midwife and a full-time university lecturer: the equivalent of two full-time jobs.

Midwifery was my life. I loved being on call for women throughout pregnancy, birthing and the first six weeks after having their baby. My passion still is to give women enough information to choose how to birth their own babies. And then I love supporting them through the early days of parenting to realise that their knowledge and instincts are superior to any book knowledge or training someone else might have. There is no blueprint or 'How-to 'guide that suits every single baby. Each mother is uniquely placed to know and meet the needs of her own child. I also had a full-time contract teaching at university to supplement the midwifery income because, at the time, we needed a mortgage, mortgage companies wouldn't even consider a mortgage to a self-employed woman!! At university, they loved having a real midwife on the staff. Women always came first, and the students loved the real-life stories that enhanced their learning.

My amazing husband, who was infinitely less passionate about his boring IT job, had gladly role-swapped and taken over the home education of our daughters, plus the washing, cooking, cleaning, shopping, mending, ironing, birthday and Christmas cards, growing veg and encouraged me to get on with what I loved.

Then…in my 50s, I realised I wasn't coping with two full-time jobs. We decided my husband could help with the income, so he set about looking for a job. We discovered, however, that he had become unemployable. I lost count of how many jobs he applied for. He wasn't even called for an interview. It was so depressing for both of us. 'Never mind,' I thought, 'I'll just retire.'

I'd had a chequered work history and thought my tiny pension pots might add up to a large enough pension to enable me to retire, so I'd set up an appointment with a pension advisor. He reviewed and re-reviewed the information before shaking his head. No, they didn't add up to much. Definitely not £2000 a month. 'All you have to do is keep going as you are, and you'll be able to retire at 85.'

I had to do something, but what? I thought about dropping the on-call, my wonderful women, and just working at the university. No, too much admin and not enough teaching. I was already biting my knuckles to keep awake during boring meetings. Anyway, not enough pay.

Drop the university, then. No, I dreaded the night calls. Births weren't so bad; it was the three hourly breastfeeding support that really took energy. Night after sleepless night, I wondered what I could do. Then, Sue turned up again at the postnatal group demonstrating her organic aloe vera products. Once more, she turned to me and said, 'You could do this. Why don't you take a look?' 'Ok,' I agreed, 'When?' Sue nearly fell off her chair. She'd asked me numerous times over five years to take a look, and I'd refused – sometimes quite rudely. How could she ask me, a professional woman, to sell products (however good they were)? I was not interested. Midwives don't sell products. Midwives don't recruit.

But here I was, agreeing to take a look!

THE RISE OF THE FEMALE ENTREPRENEUR

Complication

I'm a midwife! A professional! Do I really want to be The Aloe Vera Lady?

When Sue showed me the concept of network marketing, I was intrigued. This just might be a way to keep supporting women, helping them to birth, not a baby, but a business. It's a way to show women how to create an income for themselves and create extra income for myself by supplying excellent products. The extra 'win' here seemed to be that I didn't need to create all my income from my sales. Once I got someone started, the company would pay me an extra bonus based on her success.

Mary, a friend who refused to join me in business but is still a customer, explained it to me like this: If she, Mary, set up a hairdressing business, trained hairdressers and hired them herself, she would get an income. If that trainee, however, left and set up her own business, Mary would no longer be paid for the trainee's work. In fact, that business would be Mary's competition.

If, however, the (hypothetical) 'World of Hairdressing' were to know and acknowledge how well Mary trained her trainees and paid Mary a percentage of all the trainee's turnover, then Mary would be delighted to help her trainee to set up her own hair salon and make good money for herself, even if the trainee's salon was right across the road. Network marketing is just like that. Help someone else to be successful, and you're onto a winner. I thought maybe, just maybe, I could do that, and then the old thoughts crept back. What would people think of me, a professional, changing career so drastically – from midwife to aloe vera lady! 'Hey ho', I thought, 'just grit your teeth and get going.'

I bought the start-up box and banged it on the kitchen table at our family conference. 'We **ARE** going to use these products,' I told my husband and daughters for three months. We *will* drink aloe daily and we will replace all our current products (soap, shampoo, conditioner, etc.) If there's a matching one in the box, I want you to criticise everything.' I think I wanted them to say they were no good, which would get me off the hook. But why would I want to be let off the hook? When this was my escape route, the only way I'd found to make good money. Not just good money but a way to put in the work upfront and then retire with a great income.

The search for a company

Ah but! Had I really found the answer? If there was one network marketing company, there must be others. I went on a search. I drove my husband 'bats' while I went to business presentation after business presentation and bought start-up kit after starter kit. I checked out every single network marketing company operating in the UK at the time – 2001. There were a couple I liked the look of, but most of them didn't interest me one bit. A couple seemed to be decidedly dodgy! A friend reminded me that you'll find the good, the bad and the ugly in any industry – even the NHS.

I spent all my spare time on this research – wasted time, Sue said, but not wasted to me. To me, the search led to certainty. Certainty that I had found the best company for me and my clients. The certainty that I was working with a company with **THE** best products – well, the best aloe – available anywhere in the country, the world even (except for the actual plant grown naturally). Lots of people told me how good aloe is for all sorts of things. If so, I needed to have absolutely THE best.

By now, I'd also been able to work out company stuff that a midwife never thinks about – the security of the company, company ownership, company longevity, company values and ethics. What I learnt made me feel much more secure and in tune with the company.

One thing I was not sure about – and would not have believed had I read it in company literature – was how they treat people in the fields and factories. I was determined to visit both. Then I discovered that Forever offer an incentive that includes visiting the fields and factories! The one thing on my goal board was to win that incentive. But how?

The first sale

That's when our youngest daughter came home with an order – quite a big order – and a cheque to cover it. 'What on earth is that?' I demanded. 'It's an order, Mum! Julie's mum noticed that my skin had cleared up and asked what I was using. I told her you've started to sell aloe vera products. She was interested, so I took her a brochure and marked what I was using. She's ordered the lot.'

I was flabbergasted. 'Did you tell her how horrid the aloe is? We were nearly sick when we first started it, don't you remember?' Yes, Jenny had told her and still she wanted to try it. All my self-doubts reared their head. I did not want to sell products. I'm a midwife. I don't sell products. I don't know how to sell. And yet, here's my daughter bringing in an order.
I had to get my head around this. I needed to take stock with all of us to find out whether these aloe products had made a difference, especially since we have always used good, organic products. Discussing this at a family conference, I realised that both of our teenagers now had beautiful skin. My skin, too, was

much fresher and comfortable – I wasn't using nearly as much moisturising lotion as before. Then, the girls said their periods were not painful anymore and were not nearly so heavy. My husband said the aloe had made no difference to him, except that his back was no longer hurting all the time! I'd noticed that when I drank aloe through the night at a birth, I didn't feel anywhere near as tired the following few days. In fact, my energy was much better all the time now. And over time, we noticed that we weren't getting infections – the coughs and colds that were doing the rounds. We all agreed we felt much better, and the girls didn't want to return to their former soap, shampoo, deodorant, etc. 'Stuff,' I thought, a little bemused with myself, 'I'm selling stuff!' 'Maybe if we just talk about our own experiences with this stuff, others might want to try it.'

My 'how-to'

I still didn't really know how to go about it. Sue said to have a 'launch party', so I invited a few friends around, and she introduced the aloe and the business to them. My friends bought products, and one decided to join me in the business and bought the start-up kit. But I didn't feel comfortable with that. My sister sold Tupperware, and I definitely didn't want to do parties like that. It felt like people would be pressured to buy, and I'd lose friendships. I felt there must be a way to build a business that would work for *me*. However sociable I seem, I'm an introvert – working better with one person at a time. Groups and group work exhaust me. Time was also an issue.

I was still working full-time as a midwife with a full caseload, on-call 24/7 AND full-time in my university job. I needed to find a way to make the best use of my time while finding out whether network marketing and Forever would work for me. Aha! The company had a video. Sue said to buy 100 and post it to everyone I knew. I didn't want to spend so much money, and the whole idea made me feel sick. Instead, I decided to buy one video and use it as an excuse to catch up with friends and watch the video with them.

Here's how it went: 'Hi Jane, it's Dorothy. You know how we keep saying we'll meet for a catch-up? Let's make a date because I have a small hidden agenda I want to talk to you about– I've started a business on the side and want to show you a video. Once we've watched it, you can say 'no, not interested,' and we'll get on with our catch-up. Would that be ok?' I always got the appointment, and we always watched the video.

Once it was over, I'd immediately say, 'Thanks for watching. Now I can put a tick in my book to say I've shown it, but you're not interested.' I was truly grateful and very relieved…. And I didn't have to do any of the talking! Nearly always, they asked questions about aloe and our experience of it or about the business and how I was finding it. From this, I started to make sales, and I also began to recruit. The business started to grow in a lovely, natural way, fitting perfectly into my life and work.

The incentive trip

Remember that one goal – to visit the aloe fields and factories paid for by Forever? As I learnt to help my recruits also to sell and recruit comfortably, I noticed that my business turnover and income was growing. I was now earning enough to go part-time at the university, so I had more time to join groups to meet more people to have coffee with (and show the video)! My business grew to a point where I won the incentive to fly with my husband to America for the annual Rally. As it was our first time winning this trip, we were taken to the company offices (which were, of course, amazing) and the factory, where we met an Ethiopian woman working in the lab. I come from Ethiopia, and, as

Ethiopians do, she invited us to dinner and promised to tell us insider secrets. I was overjoyed. We'd learn what the company was like from the inside. Dinner was wonderful Ethiopian food. The secrets? I was almost disappointed that Dorcas only had praise for the company and, especially, the owner, Rex. He frequently walked around the factory talking to everyone by name and asking after their family. Everyone felt appreciated and knew their job was important.

This appreciation was underlined when we went to the aloe fields. I decided that the workers near the coach where we were dropped off would have been primed to tell us all the 'right stuff', so I determinedly set off to the other side of the huge field where I saw more workers. I assumed these would not have been primed to tell us all the good stuff about the company. I wanted the truth! I was closely followed by my husband, with the vice president of the company running after us asking if I'd like an interpreter. 'Humph,' I thought, 'I'm in America and speak the language!' It turned out that the workers were Spanish speakers.

While we were on our way, one of the workers from the other side of the field ran towards us. When he got to us, he couldn't stop shaking our hands saying, 'Thank you, thank you, thank you!' 'Thank you for what?' I asked in amazement. 'For distributing my aloe,' he replied, 'What do you mean?' I was puzzled.

'You see when I pick a really good, mature aloe leaf like this', he said, demonstrating the aloe leaf, 'its juice might go into a carton that you sell to someone. I know it will help their health. When that happens, how good do you think I feel?' I was astonished. Here was a worker in the field thinking about the health of my customers – more than I probably was!

I wondered about his name being embroidered onto his work clothes. Thinking of slave culture, I asked him about it. Stroking his embroidered name as, he replied, 'Don't you think the company is going to keep me when they have my name embroidered on four uniforms? I feel very secure in my job.' It turned out that his wife works for the company, too – and they love it. Their children have scholarships to university. The workers get more holidays than is normal in the USA, and there's a waiting list to work for the company.

A third bonus experience helped me to settle even more into working with Forever. Again, there were three examples of how special the company is. We were taken on a day out on the Colorado River in boats, then to a Forever Resort for a day of rest and recreation. Several of our party were on the boat when Rex, the company owner, joined us. We were chatting, waiting for our 'driver' as the other boats began to leave. I went to find our driver and see what was keeping him. 'Rex is supposed to be coming on our boat but hasn't arrived yet,' he said. 'Oh yes, he has,' I replied. 'We're all on and waiting for you'. It turned out that the driver hadn't driven for Forever before and was expecting an entourage with the CEO – like with other companies. He was somewhat flabbergasted that Rex is so 'normal.'

The second example at the resort was when, during an incredible banquet provided for us, I said thank you to one of the employees. 'Oh, no worries at all,' was the reply. 'Tomorrow we get a party just like this provided by the company to say thank you to us for looking after y'all!'

And the third was when we sat next to an elderly couple, John and Mary. Mary used to work in the accounts office at the resort we were visiting. One day, Rex was walking through chatting to employees when he stopped by Mary. 'Aren't you supposed to be retired?' he asked. Mary didn't have enough credits to give her a decent pension. Rex organised for her pension to be topped up so she could retire or work part-time if she chose. He also gave her and John the bungalow they were living in rent-free for as long as they wanted to live on the resort. From these experiences, I learned that Forever cares about their employees just as much as they care about and look after us, their sales force.

Consequence

I was awestruck. I can't say that I 'love' the company through and through – my family and faith come first. It is, however, a more ethical, secure, and caring company than ever I met in the NHS.

In Forever, I have been encouraged, given recognition and been appreciated. There are wonderful incentives to work for – of course there are, it's a sales company! But you don't get these in the NHS, where it doesn't matter how hard you work, you'll still get the same pay, and sometimes only recognised when you're late.

Now, if I choose to work a little harder I can increase my income – not so in the NHS where, again, you can stay late, work longer hours, work harder and get the same pay. There is no guarantee of progression. And I can't say I love sales, selling or recruiting – but I do love teaching about aloe. And I love the people I work with. I love seeing their health improve and watching them make the extra income that allows them to sleep better at night, save for a holiday or a new car. I'm not so good at setting goals for myself anymore– we have already achieved the ones I did set! Yes, I did retire from midwifery. For the last 19 years, my main income has been from Forever – even after I 'semi-retired', I've received over £1500 a month for about 4 hours of work a week.

What about you?

What do you want to achieve over the next few years?
Do you want to stay as you are?
Are you happy in your work?
Are you on the right path to achieving YOUR goals?
Or would you like a little income boost with me by your side?

And not just me – there's plenty of team and company support and training. We all want you to win.

You can relax, knowing I've done a lot of the research and asked most of the questions you'd want answers to. I know how to help introverts and extroverts, too, and how to create a business that is comfortable. It doesn't have to be a passion, but it can be enormous fun.

If you want to work it alongside your job and other responsibilities, you can do that, or you can create something big so you leave a legacy. The choice is yours.

Contact me by phone or on LinkedIn, and let's have a chat. No need to make a decision immediately – it took me five years till the time was right!
But… why wait when you can start right now?

LinkedIn: https://www.linkedin.com/in/dorothynorris/
Website: https://dorothy.flp.com/

CHAPTER 7
Janey Holliday
Mindset, life and business coach for women

Whatever you don't change, you are choosing

As I sat around a boardroom table, I thought, "What the bloody hell am I doing with my life?".

I did my degree in International Relations and wanted to be a front-line war correspondent like Kate Adie. My first job out of university was working for the government as a project manager on a PR campaign. At 22, I was preparing parliamentary questions for Tony Blair in the House of Commons. Organising high-profile media events and dealing with policy, press releases and cabinet ministers. Walking past Big Ben every morning as the sun came up was a dream and such a buzz. But two years later, when the project ended, a silly career faux pas on my part meant I found myself in marketing and PR for a TV company. One afternoon, in a meeting with the female director (who was back from maternity leave, miserable leaving her ten-month-old daughter in nursery 11 hours a day and from the commute) I found myself looking around the table, considering what you needed to do to get to the top. But for what? Is this what I really wanted for my life? Is this really success?

A few months before, whilst working in Westminster, I was at the gym. I hated exercise, but I wanted to look good! One morning, as I was plodding through a boring cross-trainer session, the step instructor ran out of the studio (that I'd never had the confidence to go in) "Right everyone, come in here and do this work out with me!" she shouted. She confessed she was hungover. She was about 40 and didn't have a perfect body or a matching gym bunny outfit. Her hair was all over the place, and she wore no make-up. But in 45 minutes, that woman changed my life and career forever. Her class was AMAZING. She was funny and kind. I enjoyed exercising for the first time in my life! She inspired me so much (the definition of inspire is to 'breathe life into' if you don't know!), and I had a real epiphany. I can still remember the routine, the music, but most importantly, that feeling.

Shortly after that boardroom wake-up call, some would say I had a moment of madness. I quit my job, sold my flat and became an aerobics instructor! Being impulsive has always been the making and breaking of me. And this one paid off! Within three months, I was teaching 26 classes a week all over the top health clubs in London. Then, I became a PT. And a few years later, I founded Fit for a Princess - outdoor workouts for women in SW London. I became known as the female fitness pioneer. I was providing fun fitness for women of all ages and abilities in a relaxing, judgement-free environment. I was named London's top health guru in 2007 and in just a few years, I'd grown a brilliant business. I hit over 300K revenue - 80% of this before 7.15 am, with 50+ women coming to classes at our peak. I became a motivational speaker. I was the first guest at the very first Stylist Magazine business event. I delivered keynotes at international fitness and business conferences. I was featured in just about every UK media, including Vogue, The Sunday Times, and I had a regular column in The Daily Mail. This was someone with no business background who used to be an exercise hater!

Remember:

- You don't need to be perfect to inspire others.
- Mistakes often lead to magic.
- Anything is possible.

Mindset is everything

It was 2 am, and I had just been physically sick from stress. I was curled up in my bathroom in floods of tears. I didn't know what I was going to do. It was September 2010. My wonderful business was going under. I'd just been through a horrendous divorce. I had become a single Mum to my twin boys at 13 months old, and they were about to turn two. I had no family in the UK. I hadn't had a full night's sleep for so long. A combination of the back end of the recession and expanding too quickly (turnover is vanity, profit is sanity became a major lesson!). The heavily discounted vouchers craze. An expensive website/e-commerce upgrade that had gone wrong. Overspending on trademarks, my business manager suddenly moving away, and me being so stretched across all areas of my life meant my business was falling apart. I was falling apart.

With over 10k a month of fixed business costs, no cash flow, and a massive drop in revenue, I had absolutely no idea how I was going to get myself out of this. It's one thing when you have time and energy to sort out big business problems. But when you don't? It was one of the darkest moments of my life. But somehow, looking back, this was actually the moment my life changed for the better. As JK Rowling once said, "Rock bottom can become the solid foundation by which you rebuild your life". In the bathroom that night, three things happened: 1) I realised that my thoughts were making a bad situation worse, and I had to change my thinking 2) I had a reality check that the business I loved was actually not a good business as a single Mum. And 3) Only ME could get me out of this!

It was the start of my journey to becoming a mindset coach. I drew a line, stopped fighting the old and started to build the new. I gathered inspirational quotes and put Post-it notes all around the house. "I can, and I will watch me", "Where you are is temporary", and "Whatever you don't change, you are choosing" became my mantras. I created vision boards of where I wanted to be—and rolled my sleeves up—challenged ALL unhelpful thinking. Focused only on solutions and worked like a dog. I compartmentalised on another level, which turned out to be my superpower as a single mum and small business owner!

I went on revenue-boosting missions, got additional childcare, and dug so deep. A typical day was a 121 at 5 am, a boot camp class at 6.15 am, then back for brekkie with my twins. I had another class at 9.30 am, worked in my home office, and had lunch with my twins. Office until 5 pm. Dinner, play and bath time. Then back out for a PT session and/or class. I worked Saturday and

Sunday mornings too. Around my work, I loved the bones of my boys and showed up as the Mum I always dreamt of being, even if the circumstances were bat shit crazy! I read every self-development book under the sun. I upgraded my mind. I kept my eyes on where I could be, not where I was. Even though it was full on, I look back on those years with a huge sense of pride.

Don't forget:

- The quality of your life depends on the quality of your thoughts.
- You choose how you show up during difficult times.
- Hard work pays off.

The sliding doors moment

Ten months later, I'd pulled my business through! But personally, I was still struggling financially. I was just about maxed out on all my credit cards. I had my twins 100% of the time. I had chosen to walk away from my marriage with absolutely nothing. Childcare costs were a killer, and I knew I needed to do something different. In July 2011, a coach I'd worked with created an online course on how to become an online coach, it was £1000. I had about £1200 spare on my credit card and I really couldn't afford it. The "Last Call!" email popped into my inbox and although I found myself saying, "I just can't afford it." Another voice appeared saying, "can you afford not to?." So, I signed up and let me tell you, I showed up on this course like NO OTHER!

I had a burning desire. If you don't know, this expression comes from a true story. An army was landing boats to recapture an island. The instructions from the captain was. "Last one off burn the boats." "What?" "Why?" everyone exclaimed! "We won't have anything to escape with if we get in trouble?". His response? "You'll fight differently when there aren't any boats!". For me, that desire then and now is mouths to feed, an inner calling to help women have a better life experience and to have a successful and enjoyable child-friendly business. There's no plan B. No boats.

My natural peak energy is very early in the morning. I'm a gazelle, as 20% of people are. So, I get way more bang for my buck before midday with my work. But 4-7 am is when I do magic. 20% are bears, the opposite. Useless before lunchtime, alive at night. 60% are tigers; slow in the morning, steady for most of the day and petering off at the end. This was where I realised the power of not only building my business around my twins but also around my energy. I would go to bed at 8 pm and get up at 4 am in order to finish my studies and build my course. I still do this now (currently, it's 4.45 am as I type this!). There is categorically no way I'd have done what I've done in my business over the years without embracing my gazelle-ness! Energy management is something I help my business clients with 12 years on. It really can be the missing link when time is tight, and there are big goals to achieve. The 9-5 fails so many on so many levels.

In September, I launched my first program. It sold out in 48 hours, and I made over £25k. In November, I launched my first 28-day online fitness boot camp, another £20k. My clients loved them. It was a total win-win. I cleared my debts and was back on track. That investment changed my life. It really was the sliding doors moment. My online business took off, and I never looked back. Since then, I've created over 25 programs and changed the lives of women all over the world.

At the end of 2012, now a mindset and life coach with an adjusted boot camp business, I moved to my dream house in Kent. The front door was exactly the same as on my vision board from 2010! When my boys started reception, I was the relaxed, happy Mum I dreamt about back in that boardroom—no commute, doing every drop-off and pick-up, and I decided to restructure my business further, allowing me to take all the school holidays off. My entire business was built around me having ten weeks off a year. When I worked, I'd often start at 4 am and kick back by 1 pm. This was my definition of success.

So:

- Never consider the cost of something, only the value.
- Have the courage to build your business around your optimum energy.
- Most small biz owners are sitting on a gold mine waiting to be found.

Plot Twist Queen and Bucket List Life

My morning coffee is one of my favourite things. But as I poured mine on the 24th of July 2015, I just didn't feel like it and squirmed. This had only ever happened once before in my life. No! I couldn't be! I was a single Mum to my nearly 7-year-old twins. I was getting no maintenance from their dad and hadn't for quite some time. And there it was… POSITIVE. WTF! When things like this happen – plot twists - something happens within me. I have this ability to stay super calm. I think it's from that bathroom moment in 2010 and having evidence that difficult things can turn out to be the very best things. Option 1 was not to have this baby. Option 2: have it. Option 1 wasn't an option for me. Option 2 wasn't an option for the father, and as I suspected, he bailed.

The quote, "When plan A is off the table, you have to thrash the hell out of plan B" became my narrative, and thrash the hell out of plan B I did. It was scary, but I knew I could do it. I dropped into trust. My twins were AMAZING. The three Musketeers became four, and my daughter was born in March 2016. No paid mat leave as a business owner! I worked up until the day she arrived and was back working when she was four days old. I remember being pregnant, thinking, how can I make money with even less time in the business? But using the Dollar V Effort concept to explore my best business options, I pivoted my offerings. I started using Facebook groups and had a fab year of business, all things considered! My clients saw how I handled this plot twist – using the mindset and life tool kit I was teaching them. They were so inspired, and I became known as the Plot Twist Queen!

But living where I was just wasn't working for me. Realising my daughter would start primary school at the same time my twins started secondary school, I started to panic. We've only got one life, right? And whatever you don't change, you are choosing, and so, with that impulsive nature of mine, I decided to go on a different life path. I always had 'living by the sea' on my bucket list and thought fuck it, why not now? So, I moved to Sidmouth, Devon! By myself! With my three kids in tow (then 8,8 & 1). Having never been there before, I didn't even know one person there! People said, "Aren't you scared?" but honestly, the fear of the unknown became MUCH less than the fear of staying where I was unhappy.

The benefits of running an online business came to fruition on another level (you see that sliding door investment was STILL showing up!). I can now live anywhere, and we became the beach crew! It was the best decision ever. But that first year was the happiest and hardest of my life. My live-in childcare who I'd meticulously interviewed months before moving, pulled out five days before

I moved - agh! So, there I was; business owner, single Mum, baby, no friends, no family nearby, no childcare! Mental doesn't cover it. I had to borrow money into my business to give myself some breathing space and get by with compromised childcare. It was far from ideal, but we got through it. My ability to compartmentalise my life continued to be my saving grace. In fact, my ability to be where my feet are and not take stress or difficulty into other parts of my life – both in and out of business is my superpower, and it can be yours too.

Remember:

- When plot twists happen, put your focus on what you CAN control and let go of the rest.
- The magic you're looking for is often the other side of fear.
- Your bucket list life is waiting for you!

Square peg, round hole

At three years old, my daughter wasn't talking and could only be described as a tornado allergic to sleep! She ran everywhere, hated being inside and had no off button. She was diagnosed with autism (and since then, sensory processing disorder and ADHD). A 'square peg in a round hole system', I was told. Another plot twist on another level! My daughter is the most phenomenal human being I've ever had the pleasure of knowing. We were destined to be mother and daughter. And my relationship with her is the thing I'm most proud of in my life. She needs a lot. I give a lot.

I have her 100% of the time. I get no maintenance. She can't be looked after by many people, nor for very long. The SEN system is atrocious, and it can be so overwhelming. But THANK GOD I'm a mindset coach! And a time block ninja, and instead of complaining, and saying, 'I've got no time' and living with fear. I parent from a place of trust. I triage my business and life. I compromise with good grace, and just do what I can. There are so many gaps, and there is always more I can do in my business. But there is only so much of me. I have an affirmation I say every evening; "Janey, you are enough, and you've done enough".

In September 2023 (now a chatterbox at 7!), she was going through hell at school. She had been finding it hard for some time. I had home education at the back of my mind, as something I'd probably have to do in the next couple of years. For me, mental health and shining bright come way above (and not from) academic qualifications. Too many awesome people leave school with no confidence, no self-worth, or no awareness of their unique power, oblivious to their incredible capabilities and their soul completely crushed. NOT MY CHILD!

I remember the moment so clearly. She had been crying non-stop since 3.30 am and still had tears rolling down her face as I drove her to school. I looked at her and said, "I'll get you out of this, I promise you. I just need a little bit more time to get my business to a place where I can take you out". She looked up. I will never ever forget her face. She believed me. She was relying on me. But she needed me to do it now. Could I? I really needed more time. But if I had to, maybe I could make it work. I cried all the way to the gym, as I often did after a brutal drop-off. My gut instinct was screaming, "Be brave, do it!" and after another car crash of a day with her needs not being met, that was it. I couldn't do it to her anymore. I couldn't do it to me.

You're only as happy as your unhappiest child. Plan A was off the table, and it was time to thrash the hell out of plan B.

I deregistered my daughter from school, and that night, for the first time in 7.5 years, she slept through the night! I didn't know how I'd run my business with even less time, but I trusted myself. My priority was to increase cash flow to keep me calm. Off to the local spa I went, with a rhino desk pad and got my business hat on. I wanted to create something authentic, easy for me to put together, that would give me a fast revenue boost. I wrote £15,000 in 6 weeks at the top of the pad, and I brainstormed all the ways I could do it. Two hours later, I'd put together "Turn Your Life Around in a Year," that sat in between my membership and 121s, and went on to do an 18k month!

Home education has turned out to be the best thing ever. We love it. It has made me look at my business AND life differently, and I'm realising very quickly that the big blocks we think we have in life might actually be our greatest assets and opportunities. You just have to lean in, decide not to be a victim of your circumstances and open your mind to make things work, I've chosen to see this next chapter of my business and life, as one big adventure, and I've turned what some would deem something really stressful into something truly liberating, and that is the power of mindset.

Finally:

- See barriers as hurdles and GET OVER THEM!
- Reframing can turn any situation around.
- When you have to, you usually can… burn those boats!

Janey Holliday, AKA The Women's Mindset coach and founder of The Women's Mindset Club and Women's Mindset Business Club

Website: www.janeyholliday.com

THE RISE OF THE FEMALE ENTREPRENEUR

CHAPTER 8
Charlotte Dover
Coach and mentor to late diagnosed ADHD women and founder of (Maybe) ADHD

Moments of utter despair

I had it all. The loving partner. The beautiful home. Career success. An income which allowed me to do most of the things I wanted to do. The supportive family and friends.

So why was I standing in the shower, crying uncontrollably, thinking, "I can't keep doing this"?

Despite all appearances to the contrary, I was deeply unhappy. I was REALLY good at my job, working in property. I exceeded all expectations and targets and was earning a nice income. But I hated it, and it made me feel "less-than" and miserable every day.

Despite having "friends", I felt lonely all the time, and I was aware that I wasn't being the kind of partner I wanted to be. I didn't have the energy to do anything but talk about how much I hated work, or crash out in front of the TV with several glasses of wine and crap food, meaning it was no surprise I was also uncomfortable with how I looked and felt in my body.

The answer to why I was so unhappy didn't come until several years later, September 2020 to be precise… and it wasn't anything I had EVER considered… but before we get to that, let's backtrack to sobbing in the shower.

Well, actually, let's go back even further than this because it might help set the scene.

The first 35 years

Ever since I can remember, I felt like I didn't "fit."

I always felt on the outside of friendship groups. Like I was allowed to be there but was not really part of them as someone who was really wanted or would be missed, never feeling important to anyone.

At school, I was bullied and appeared to be a magnet for people who liked to control others, and I found myself confused and sad a lot of the time. This meant from a relatively young age, I looked for love and acceptance in ways which weren't healthy for me and left me feeling even worse. I'd throw myself into relationships. Moulding myself into what I thought my current partner would want, but ending up broken hearted and losing a piece of myself every time.

Throughout my 20s and early 30s, I had terrible relationships with food and alcohol, using them as coping mechanisms and more than once putting myself in unsafe situations.

I felt deeply ashamed of myself and who I was.
For not being happy and wanting something "more".
Ashamed I had no control over my eating and drinking.

That I constantly let myself down, had no willpower, and seemed unable to manage my finances either, chucking it all into buying stuff to make myself feel better. And my house…I couldn't keep it tidy, which I felt shame around every single day.

But on the surface, it seemed like I had it all lined up. I became BRILLIANT at putting on a brave face. Saying everything was great. No one ever saw the chaos in my house because I worked so hard to tidy up whenever we had visitors, and no one ever saw the chaos in my head because I always had a smile on my face around others (apart from my poor husband). There were no outward signs of my deep unhappiness. My career was a big factor in that unhappiness. Despite being good at my job, I now understand that it wasn't suited to my individual values and strengths. Over time, this mismatch wore me down until I just couldn't do it any longer.

Ironically, it was being made redundant, one of the hardest things I've ever had to navigate and one which took me years to make peace with, that helped me realise I needed to leave the industry I was in and to be brave and go it alone as a self-employed coach. I'd spent YEARS (and hours and £1000s) on my training in a desperate quest to help myself feel better. Now it was time to use it!

OK, you're a coach, so now what?

I believed that because I saw so many people around me saying it, that establishing myself as a coach would be easy. Clients would come to me just because of my training.

But they didn't (and sadly, there are 100s of irresponsible coach training schools and courses selling a dream lifestyle of working part-time, from anywhere and making as much money as you want. It does NOT come that easily just because you've qualified).

I don't want that to discourage anyone thinking of training as a coach, it's incredibly rewarding, but please go in with your eyes open. Building a business takes time and dedication, and it's a lot easier when you do it in a way that works WITH your unique skills, values and strengths.

It took me five years from starting training as a coach to be able to begin building the business I have now. And had I not been on a particular business group call 3 ½ years ago, I still wonder what might have happened or not…

This was my "mic drop" moment.

A fellow member was talking about her clients and the struggles they were facing. She was describing me. The clients she supported were late-diagnosed ADHD women. And at that moment, I knew. This was me too.

It wasn't a "wondering". It was a bone-deep KNOWING that this was the missing piece of my puzzle. Until this point, like so many did and still do... I thought ADHD was something which only affected children and, mainly boys. Yet despite this, I was certain this was the thing I had been struggling to understand my whole life.

Diagnosis and self-discovery

I won't go deeply into my diagnosis experience, as it could take up the whole chapter, but within six months, I had a confirmed diagnosis of (combined) ADHD. This was incredibly validating and self-affirming but, at the same time, opened up a whole new can of worms.

I was given an "answer" by way of a confirmed diagnosis but no answers or guidance as to what I should do with the knowledge. So there I was; EVERYTHING had changed, but at the same time, nothing had changed at all.

So what did I do? I got on with it. I took the answer I was given and went about life as though nothing had actually changed. I was ecstatic because I finally understood why I'd been feeling so utterly useless, lazy and broken my whole life, and that it wasn't my fault.

I thought that that would be enough.

It wasn't... I can't remember much about the following eight months, which is a sign in itself, but I do know that it led to the biggest mental health crash I'd ever had in my life.

If I thought crying in the shower before work was bad, this well-being nosedive turned into days of crying (NYE 2021 was my worst day; I cried in bed for hours, unable to get up). I felt helpless and hopeless. Rather than feeling empowered and positive about what I'd learned, it had totally turned my already shaky self-concept on its head.

I hadn't been prepared for the complex rollercoaster of emotions which came alongside diagnosis. Yes, there was elation, but there was also confusion, disappointment, self-doubt and grief for the version of myself I had to let go of. Any hopes of being neurotypical, being the kind of person who didn't forget things, had to put so much effort into the most basic things in life and didn't always feel like I was the odd one out, vanished.

This version of me wasn't on the table anymore, and the impact of this realisation was crushing. I thought that knowing what was going on for me would be the key, but it turned out I didn't know what lock to put it in.

But I'm here, with a chapter in this book about the rise of the female entrepreneur, and I couldn't be prouder of myself for being right here right now, given the despair I felt just a couple of years ago.

Finding the gateway

Part of the reason the months following my diagnosis were so hard was that I didn't expect things would have to change. I thought that just knowing I was

ADHD was enough. But instead, I carried on trying to do things the same way as I always had.

When you have a brain which works differently from the majority of other peoples', it can be soul-destroying, seeing others easily doing things you find almost impossible. Seeing them achieving the things you want to achieve faster than you are, seeing their successes you're working SO hard to achieve.

During my years of "trying to get my business to work", I've spent 1000s hours and £s (many) on programmes promising to create leads, six-figure businesses, passive income, an unbreakable funnel etc. You might have expected this to stop post-diagnosis, but my self-doubt was so high that I leaned even MORE into trying to find the solution to "fix" myself and my business problems.

I worked with therapists, which left me feeling like I couldn't even do therapy right (it turns out that even therapists who specialise in ADHD often don't always know how to hold space for ADHDers). I bought numerous courses and programmes and spent an amount that still makes me feel sick on a business coach who wasn't able to work with my busy brain. Rather than her suggesting this wasn't the right fit, we limped along, which left me feeling incompetent and even more helpless for six months, with no money left to be able to get the help I really needed.

It went so far that I believed to be a successful coach, I needed to do a psychology degree (I had actually already studied psychology at university as part of a combined degree) to be "good enough". I still look back at this time of my life with sadness and compassion for the woman I was, desperately needing a lifeline but not knowing how to give it to myself.

But I refused to give up. I knew I had to start doing things differently, as nothing was going to change for me unless I started to see things through an ADHD lens and work <u>with</u> my brain instead of against it.

As soon as I began to do this, I realised how capable I was of helping myself when I did it MY WAY. I grew in self-belief and self-compassion and started to trust myself.

This was the lock I needed to put my diagnosis key into. Finally, it clicked and turned. It didn't suddenly make everything easy, but I did know now that I could back myself to navigate challenges, no matter how squiggly a path I took or how slow the progress.

This was the turning point for me, personally and professionally, and it was from this point I began to build a strong foundation as an ADHD woman and business owner.

Putting the puzzle back together

The more I used this "ADHD lens", the more I understood why none of the courses, coaching, tips, programmes and "guru" advice had worked for me.

The vast majority of the information and support came from neurotypical brains who often find the things I find hard much easier / no big deal, including being consistent, being able to separate their logical "business mind" from their emotional self, and using motivation, willpower and traditional goal setting to progress.

For me and the vast majority of the ADHD women I support, this approach to entrepreneurship doesn't work.

Our brains don't work in the same way when it comes to willpower, motivation, risk and reward, so when we try to apply the rules and strategies we see others (seemingly) able to implement with ease, guess what happens…

We blame ourselves if we don't find it easy. We decide we're not good enough, motivated enough, dedicated enough or that we don't want it enough. We feel frustrated, self-doubt starts to run the show, and we want to throw everything in the bin.

This happens to so many of us, and I've lost count of the number of times I've said, "I can't keep doing this" about growing my business. But I'm resilient and determined to problem solve and find my way.

Resilience is a common and strong ADHD trait. We often have to learn this from an early age as life can feel so painful and disappointing for us from when we first become aware of how we interact with the world around us. As a note, this may be true for the vast majority of humans, but with ADHD, all the human things we experience are magnified, so every disappointment, rejection, challenge, feeling of being different or ashamed can hit us HARD and even derail us for days.

This is linked to something called Rejection Sensitive Dysphoria (RSD), which can mean you experience rejection so strongly it can feel like physical pain. This is one of the main challenges I help my (Maybe) ADHD clients within the world of entrepreneurship; putting yourself out there and risking rejection is a daily occurrence and one we want to run and hide from!

Much of the traditional self-help and business advice is written by and for neurotypical brains. It focuses on if you "just" do these things, then you'll be successful, but this doesn't work for those of us with ADHD brains.

So what do we do?

Hard as it seems, I've learned that when it comes to building a business which aligns with my hopes, values, and capacity, I have to work with my energy, my interests, and my consistent inconsistency.

If I'm not 100% "into" an idea, I'm basically out. All energy expended on it is going to feel like a monumental effort. I HAVE to trust my brain sparks and my gut and figure out my own way of doing things. Because trying to copy what others have done leads nowhere but frustration and burnout for me.

It was only once I decided I'd had enough of feeling hopeless, like I was failing at everything I tried to do and figured out what my actual capacity for showing up on my best and worst days (and weeks) looked like that I stopped comparing myself to others and looked at doing the best for myself.

In January 2022, a very wise lady who has also written a chapter in this book (Andrea Rainsford) told me that niching into ADHD coaching would help me build a strong business. But at that point, I knew I wasn't ready to do this. My impostor syndrome was at an all-time high, and I was only a few months into feeling better after my post-diagnosis crash.

I knew I needed to keep on understanding myself and this brilliant brain of mine so I could step into the ADHD coaching world with the confidence that I understood how to navigate life with a brain which works the way mine does.

And in January 2023, after 35 years of living with undiagnosed ADHD and three years of knowing, it was finally time for me to do this.

All the pieces came together, and I've been able to build a business which is fulfilling, provides me with the income I need, and is in line with my values. It helps life feel better for others who, like me, are realising they aren't lazy, broken or stupid, they are, in fact (Maybe) ADHD.

The growth of (Maybe) ADHD

In the past 12 months, I have grown my voice and visibility as a trusted ADHD professional. I know who I am, I know what I stand for, and I understand how I operate. I've undertaken training and research which enables me to support others who are going through similar experiences to my own.

Unfortunately, we are in a national crisis when it comes to accessing assessments for ADHD. Demand far exceeds the capacity in the NHS, and wait times are becoming longer and longer.

I want to help those who can't currently access a formal assessment and diagnosis still feel seen, heard and validated.

This is why (Maybe) ADHD was born. We can't know for 100% sure that people who haven't been assessed by a qualified diagnostician have ADHD, but we CAN recognise the struggles and challenges common with ADHD. We can't diagnose, but we can work on the assumption that you are at least "maybe" ADHD.

I now provide support and resources for all budgets; free downloads, a free community, self-led courses, a private membership for further support and small group coaching programmes. I also offer 1-1 coaching with me or one of my associate coaches for both private clients and those claiming the Access to Work Grant (no formal diagnosis required).

This grant exists in England, Scotland and Wales to help people with disabilities and differences get into and stay in work. It provides funding for all sorts of things, from software, to specialist equipment and human support, including neurodiversity coaching.

Unfortunately, the application process itself is a barrier for many ADHD people, and the grants awarded are inconsistent, frustrating and often seem unfair.

My mission is to create a place that makes accessing the grant and getting the support you need easier. By supporting people through the process and levelling the coaching field so that whatever your coaching award is, we're able to provide you with the same high-quality support.

Wherever you are in your journey of exploring your neurodivergence, we're here to provide support, guidance and fact-based information. This is the support I wish I'd had on my own path from despair to carving out a 'me-shaped' place in this world, loving what I do and knowing I make a difference to the lives of people who need it.

You can be a leader AND a learner at the same time

To this day, I'm often not 100% sure if my feelings, my preferences, and my thoughts are mine and mine alone because I've spent decades moulding myself into what I believed I needed to be.

What I AM 100% sure of is that I have the self-awareness to recognise this and trust myself to navigate it, no matter what life throws at me. Every day helps me learn more about myself.

I can only look back now and wonder what would have happened if I was still trying to shame, force and berate myself into doing things the way others told me was the "right" way to do it.

Without my diagnosis, without fully embracing doing things my own way (even with self-doubt coming along for the ride!) I wouldn't be where I am now.

This is what I want for each and every one of you: ADHD, Neurodivergent, Neurotypical, or however you express yourself or experience life. I can't promise it's an easy road to travel, but it's the most rewarding and courageous thing you can do for yourself, and those around you.

This is why my coaching work and the (Maybe) ADHD community exists. To provide a safe space for you to be seen, heard, understood, accepted and welcomed. We're here to believe in you until you feel brave enough to see yourself as the brilliant, resourceful and capable woman you already are.

If you're curious about ADHD, to learn more for yourself and explore its impact on your life or to understand it better so you can support those you care

THE RISE OF THE FEMALE ENTREPRENEUR

about, then I invite you with open arms to connect with me and explore my part of this neurodiverse world.

You can find all my contact details, see more information about what I do and access resources and more by following the below link:

www.charlottedover.com/everythingpage

Alternatively, contact me here:

Email: charlotte@charlottedover.com

LinkedIn: https://www.linkedin.com/in/charlotte-dover-coaching/

Instagram: https://www.instagram.com/maybe_adhd_/

CHAPTER 9
Aneeta Marshall Law
Headhunter and Career Strategist

I'm Aneeta, the MD of Parker Harris Ltd, a recruitment for recruitment consultancy that focuses on the education and healthcare recruitment markets. I have enjoyed building my business as it has allowed me to raise a family and support them in their long-term goals and achievements. Furthermore, it has allowed me to spend more time with them and watch them mature and develop into amazing young adults.

Who was I before Parker Harris?

I was born and raised in North London. My mother is mixed Vietnamese and Indian, and my father is an Indian Malaysian. My mother had a strong academic background and attended university, attaining a master's in European History and French Lit. My father was a badminton coach and had a few small businesses, including a sports shop. At the tender age of twelve, I was too young to serve the public, so I spent my time in the stockroom stringing racquets. If I wasn't at school, home, or working, I was playing badminton, and I still play to this day.

My parents had a very difficult relationship and got divorced when I was young. This resulted in Mum having to raise myself and my older brother alone. It was a struggle, regardless of her academics and ability to speak four languages she was seen as a foreigner and as such, was poorly paid. However, she made it work and ensured that my brother and I had a roof over our heads, clothes on our backs and food in our stomachs. Looking back, I have nothing but admiration for my mother and the way she coped with what life threw at her. She drummed it into us that we had to strive to be the best at whatever we did and never put ourselves in a position where we had to rely on anyone for anything, she wanted more for us. I didn't really appreciate at the time how hard things were, even when she had no choice but to put me into care to keep me safe for a while. I can't believe how hard that must have been for her. My mum always had the highest level of respect for highly educated people and desperately wanted me to go down the academic route, which meant no socialising, just studying, which I didn't enjoy as I was forced to do it. Many years later, I discovered I was dyslexic.

Growing up in the 70s and 80s as a person of colour was extremely difficult. My parents were strict, and I had very little freedom. The clothes I wore were clean and in good condition but were dated. This made me feel like a total outsider and very lonely. All the girls in my year had the latest fashions and nice hairstyles, wore makeup and were allowed to meet up after school. I wasn't jealous of them and what they did. I was just extremely angry that my life was so different from theirs. Don't get me wrong, I had friends, some of which are my best friends to date, but it was extremely hard being accepted as the Indian girl in a Catholic school. I hated school. Unlike my brother who went to university and became a child protection officer after graduating, I left school at 15 with no qualifications because I didn't sit my GCSEs. Life at this point had become extremely traumatic, and after living in care for a while, I then lived by myself in a flat in Tottenham.

My career options were severely limited, but I knew I wanted a better life than the one I had lived so far. I knew that money was the only thing that could affect change, and I was keen to make that happen. The only skills I had were a natural inquisitiveness and the ability to communicate with people. The problem I had was how to combine the two and get a career that wasn't hinged on my lack of qualifications or the colour of my skin.

Like many people, I stumbled into a sales role. I sold Industrial cleaning chemicals to any company that had machines that needed cleaning fluid. I sold timeshare holidays in London and in Spain. I also sold publishing and advertising space. I guess the real eye-opener for me was selling timeshares. I loved the thrill of selling in a highly competitive environment. There were 20 salespeople selling every day, and I wanted to be in the top 3; the loud music, bright pictures on the walls, and talk of worldwide luxury holidays all added to the day's excitement. To top it all off, I met some amazing people. A typical sales pitch could last anything from 3 hours to 9 hours. It was by far the hardest job, but it was fun, even if some of the people were incredibly rude. What made it really appealing for me was that it didn't matter if I was dyslexic or that I did not have any qualifications. It was all about verbal communication, and I'm pretty good at that. There I was, 20 years old with four years of sales experience under my belt and a real hunger to make good money. I read an advert in the paper where a small recruitment agency in north London wanted to hire a recruitment consultant—no experience was required except a background in sales.

My recruitment journey began with Rolodex cards and three temps sitting at my desk in the morning, waiting for me to call around all my clients to get them to work that day. I remember doing the payroll by hand for 150 temps, all coming in to collect their paychecks on a Friday afternoon; then, they would not bother to go back to work in the afternoon and go to the pub instead, which sent my clients into a frenzy.

Why I started Parker Harris

I started Parker Harris because I wanted to be successful off my own merit. I wanted to make a salary that would allow me to live the life that I wanted. A life that would make my traumatic past and lack of education become totally irrelevant. A life that involved a loving husband and, fingers crossed, a child or two.

As a young woman of mixed heritage who had a traumatic upbringing, it wasn't easy fitting into any work environment. I had to ignore all the isms that were thrown at me. The racism, the sexism, and the 'you cannot do this' ism. I wanted to react in the worst way but knew it would not fare well for me. I knew I had the determination to be successful, and the only way to rise above the isms was to be successful in what I was doing. I realised that a good recruiter develops relationships while a brilliant recruiter ensures those relationships produce a profit by delivering a great service and not letting those relationships sour by under-delivering.

I understood how to create a recruitment pipeline and produce solid results. No matter what company I worked for, my billings spoke for themselves and allowed me to rise above the quagmire of plodders and one-hit wonders. I was focused and wouldn't let anything stop me from earning as close to a six-figure salary as possible. It was all too easy to get distracted in an office environment, so I ignored the office banter and concentrated on closing deals, and I became extremely proficient at it. This approach made me a lot of money and allowed me to live how I wanted to. I bought my first home at 21, got married, went on exotic holidays, and shopped in Bond Street. What more could a girl from Wood Green ask for?

After years spent working for recruitment agencies focusing on the commercial sector, I was offered the opportunity to work for a start-up recruitment for recruitment agency. So, from placing secretarial support staff, I went on to place IT Recruiters. In my first year, I billed in excess of £250K. In my second year, I doubled that figure and had made a name for myself in the industry. My employers were happy with my work, but I felt under-valued, and I knew that I had a lot more to offer. Although I was offered a management position, I knew that I wanted to start a family, and the two wouldn't combine.

It would require me to live in two worlds, and I knew from speaking with parents that my children could potentially grow up not seeing as much of me as I would like. My mum worked so hard to raise myself and my brother, and I didn't want to experience the struggle that she went through either. I needed an opportunity that would allow me to have a family while still earning at a level I was used to. It was then that the idea of working for myself really hit me. If I could open a company and bill consistently, then that would allow me to turn my dream into reality. So, in 2000, I bit the bullet, and Parker Harris was formed.

How I started Parker Harris

The idea of running your own business is a scary concept for many; it certainly was for me. Going from a great base salary and commission in a company that had a marketing, IT and HR department to working on commission only was a space I never thought about being in again. Let's face it, if I didn't bill, I wouldn't earn, so it was commission only. I wasn't about to go and work for someone else, so I had to make it work. I had to dig deep in order to stay motivated and keep my focus. It wasn't going to be an easy ride, but I was certainly up for the challenge.

I tried to create a plan for success. I tried, but I had no experience of business planning, so I did what I knew. I picked up the phone and started speaking to people who wanted to hire. Luckily, I had made some valuable relationships and was recommended to other companies. I knew I had to make my service different, and I knew I had to go above and beyond in order to retain these big names. So, I made myself accessible. This meant taking calls up until 10 pm 7 days a week, allowing candidates and clients the time to explain what they wanted and me the time to advise them on who they should hire or who they should be working for in their next role.

The next two years were a roller coaster with more ups than downs, I was making placements hand over fist and really enjoying the success I had created. I was working with the most prestigious names in IT Recruitment and making at least five to six placements per month. I remember creating my first invoice and thinking, "I did that for me, all by myself", and the buzz I got from it was amazing. It gave me confidence and peace of mind. I knew I was capable of deciding my own future with hard work and determination.

I sat back and was pleased with what I had achieved, but I knew that things were about to change. The IT sector suffered a massive blow, and agencies were downsizing, which meant business started to suffer. I had more candidates calling me than ever, and I didn't have enough roles to place them into. The once successful sector was now a shambles, and nothing on the horizon said it would get better. Yes, it survived after a time, but I couldn't afford to weather the storm, so I had to change direction to survive. I studied other market sectors and decided that Healthcare and Education were the most attractive sectors. Schools always need teachers, and hospitals need medical staff, so agencies in those sectors would always need consultants and managers.

This meant reinventing Parker Harris, and trying to get a credible reputation in a sector that was spearheaded mainly by ex-teachers who had set up their own agencies, or medical agencies that really needed game changers and strong leaders. Luckily for me, the tide was turning, both sectors were gaining attention for their growth potential. Recruiters from other markets wanted a piece of the action, and I was now in a position to help them achieve that while at the same time giving the agencies that I worked with business-minded consultants who knew how to grow a profitable desk.

The consultants that worked in these sectors were a far cry from the IT recruiters that I had been dealing with over the years who wanted high base salaries along with a Porsche as their company car. Not all of them were like that, but there were quite a few. The candidates in these sectors wanted companies who had a great reputation and companies where they could progress if successful. It was a real struggle in the beginning. Getting my head around public sector recruitment and gaining a real understanding of how each agency operated individually. Even the large players in the sector had different ways of recruiting depending on the branch locations and the local decision-makers. With some clients, I was successful, with others I was just another recruitment for recruitment agent.

So, I went through a steep learning curve, but I knew that I had to be different. Especially considering the amount of recruitment for recruitment businesses that had now sprung up and were targeting the same sectors. I redefined my service, and rather than just making placements, I started advising professionals on their long-term career plans. This led me to start working at a senior level within a number of recruitment businesses. It allowed me to gain a deeper understanding of my candidate's career goals and my client's growth plans. It was a very difficult journey to undertake.

What does Parker Harris Do?

Parker Harris is now a leading recruitment for recruitment company within the education and healthcare sectors. My hard work and service delivery over the years has earned me an enviable reputation and a lot of respect from both my clients and my competitors. I'm now in a position where I can choose who I would like to work with based on the relationships that have been forged over the last 20 years of making successful placements. Placements that have enhanced an individual's career or have increased a company's profit through introducing talented managers and big billing consultants.

Over the years, I have also recruited for the operational areas of a client's business, including HR, Payroll and Compliance. This is a massive compliment as it shows that my clients really trust my judgement, and it allows me to interact with all facets of the business. I enjoy learning new things. Even with my experience, every day can produce a learning curve of one description or another. Speaking with recruiters in the morning and then interviewing a HR director in the evening means that I must wear different hats and use all the skills and experience acquired over the years.

This all sounds very serious and profit-focused. It paints a picture of a money-mad woman hell-bent on being successful at any cost and one who wants all the cake to eat. It could not be further from the truth. I love what I do as the people I work with often only work with me because they like me; luckily, I like them as well. In fact, some have crossed the line and become very good friends. I've dealt with some clients for over 20 years, and I hope to continue to do so. I am open and honest with them, they trust my point of view because I always strive to do the correct thing. If you heard me on the phone to most of my clients, you would think they were personal calls and not business related. I have laughed with them, and I have cried with them. I have been an emotional support and confidant when required.

It has not all been plain sailing, far from it. I still have days filled with stress and nights where my mind won't rest because so much is at stake. I have awoken in the morning to deals that had been confirmed the day before, only for the candidate to accept a counteroffer. I get a sick feeling in my gut, and all the work that I have put into filling that position has amounted to nothing. On top of that, I have a disappointed client, and I am back to square one with that vacancy. I take pride in my work, and it makes you question yourself when things don't go as you expect them to. That said, recruitment is a people industry, and people change their mind all the time. I have heard every reason under the sun as to why things don't work out, and it still frustrates me. I still tell myself, "Put on your big girl pants and soldier on. These candidates are not going to place themselves".

The key elements of success at Parker Harris are the ability to listen, understand and act. I have never believed in pushing a square plug into a round hole, and unless you truly understand what you are doing, then you run the risk of doing it badly. Success is never an overnight thing, it is something that is developed and nurtured over time. I've had losses and failures, but I have always taken the time to learn from each experience in order to avoid them where possible.

Opening Parker Harris has also given me the ability to devote my spare time when it's available to volunteer within my local community. I was a Brownies leader for three years, and my name was Raven. I was a Vice Chairperson for the PTA at my children's school and assisted at functions to raise money, and more recently, I helped set up a local community fridge/ foodbank, which I'm actively involved in. I really do have a soft side and a very thick empathic vein running through me. Over the years, I have semi-adopted (unofficially) two young individuals and guided them in their personal life and professional lives. Seeing them turn into successful young adults has been a very rewarding experience.

Life has been a real journey, and I am very proud of where I am today. I'm happily married, and my husband supports me in everything I do. My greatest achievement is being a mum to our twins, Joshua and Bailey, who were born in 2005. Joshua is now studying for his MEng degree in computer science (my mum is over the moon), and Bailey is currently studying to be a chef while working at Cambridge University. I'm also blessed to have some amazing friends.

In retrospect, it's not been easy; some events had me holding that towel up in the air, ready to throw it onto the canvas. However if I could travel back in time and speak to the younger me I would tell her you are bold, you are brave, never give up, you've got this. Yes, it's going to be scary and frightening at times, but it's absolutely going to be worth it.

If you've resonated with the journey of Parker Harris and are seeking an education and healthcare rec for rec consultant who goes beyond the ordinary, then look no further, experience matters, relationships matter, and results matter. So, what I want to convey is quite simple – "Bloody hell, give me a bell!" Why? Because you won't find anyone better suited to understand your needs, connect with your vision, and deliver exceptional results.

Here's why reaching out to me is the next logical step: Proven Track Record: With over 24 years in the industry, my hard work and service delivery have garnered an enviable reputation. The success stories of placements enhancing careers and increasing companies' profits speak volumes.

Trust and Relationship: Clients trust my judgement to recruit. It's more than a professional relationship; it's about trust, openness, and understanding.

Adaptability and Expertise: Wearing different hats throughout the day, I bring a wealth of experience, adaptability, and a commitment to what makes me successful – listening, understanding, and taking action.

If you would like to get in contact with me you can find me on LinkedIn at: **linkedin.com/in/aneeta-marshall-law-8588b915**

CHAPTER 10
Gemma Howorth
Virtual Assistant & VA Coach

Hi, I'm Gemma, Virtual Assistant business owner and VA coach. I help overwhelmed entrepreneurs and CEOs go from chaos to calm with my virtual business support, time management sessions and accountability packages. As a VA Coach, I help new and aspiring Virtual Assistants to start and scale their own business through my Power Hour sessions and CPD Accredited course.

I always knew the 9 – 5 life wasn't for me

I never really knew what I wanted to do when I was growing up. I found this frustrating at times! I wasn't afraid to work hard, landing my first weekend job at 13. I had the determination and willingness to dive into a career path, but the problem was, I just didn't know where to direct it.

I was a very headstrong child and was born with a love for animals. From a very early age, I would raise money and donate to animal charities. I remember my first adopted animal, Bubbles the dolphin, whose picture was stuck on my wardrobe throughout my childhood. At ten years old, I would get up early on a Saturday morning and volunteer at a local cat rescue. By 11, I made the decision to stop eating meat. I remember sitting at school eating a ham sandwich and thinking, 'Why am I eating a pig!' and decided from that moment I would never eat meat again! When some of my family teased me, saying they didn't believe that I would stick to it, this only made me more determined; I wanted to prove them wrong! I have never eaten meat since!

My dream was to have lots of land and rescue animals, but as that wasn't exactly going to happen any time soon, I had to decide what path to take when I left school.

Becoming an entrepreneur was never considered as an option. Going into employment was just seen as the thing to do, so I decided to go with my organisation skills and landed my first full-time position working in an office. This started my experience and development of skills in all areas of administration and PA work. I loved organising everything, working through a good to-do list, spotting areas for improvement and seeing results!

I met my husband when I was 15 years old, and when I turned 19, we got our first house together. I realise that this sounds young, but it didn't feel that way at the time. I suppose I have always been quite mature for my age, so when we came back from holiday and saw a house for sale, this spurred us on to take the next step. We got married when I was 22 years old. With organisation being what I am good at, I got to work planning our special day. I had an image of my ideal venue in mind; I wanted to get married within the grounds of a beautiful hotel overlooking the sea. After searching, I found the exact venue that I had visualised! A beautiful venue in Cyprus.

Back to work, whilst working in a law firm, I was offered the chance to train as a solicitor. I discussed this with my husband, who thought that it was an amazing opportunity and encouraged me to take it. However, it didn't feel right, it wasn't something that I was passionate about, yes, the money would be good, but would I be excited to go to work every day? - probably not, so I turned it down. It just didn't feel like the path for me. I knew that we would be trying to start a family soon and that my whole working life would change.

Freedom & Flexibility

At age 25 and pregnant with my first child, I knew that the 9-5 life would just not work for me with a baby. I had friends who paid almost their whole wage to a nursery, and I was determined to take a different path. So, after maternity leave, I went back to work part-time. While splitting my week between work and spending time with my son was great, I soon realised I needed more income. I was adamant that I would not give up time with my baby, so when I saw an opportunity to join a network marketing company where I could earn a flexible income, I decided to give it a try!

I am an all-in kind of girl, so I totally threw myself into my new venture and was surprised by how well it took off. This was back in 2011, a time when many people hadn't heard of network marketing. I only knew a couple of people who had done anything like this before, so being slightly sceptical, I didn't really expect it to amount to much. I assumed that I would join, get some products, and be left to it on my own. I was wrong and soon fell in love with the supportive, empowering community that I had walked into. A fire really had been lit inside of me! I loved how I could control my income and earn flexibly around my child; this was so different to the corporate world that I was used to! I was bringing onboard other mums like me and loved to help them do the same. After one year in the business, I hit my first leader promotion, and it continued to grow. In January 2014, whilst pregnant with my second child, I was able to say goodbye to the 9-5 life. Redundancies were being made at the office where I worked part-time, so I volunteered and took this as a universal nudge to leave the corporate world. Was this scary? Absolutely, my income was now totally in my hands, so I made a promise to myself to do everything I could to make it work. Knowing that it is all down to you is both frightening and empowering at the same time! It pushes you to level up!

This was it, 29 years old, four months pregnant and out of the 9-5 world for good!

My daughter was born one month after my 30th birthday. The business that I had built, selling products, and developing my team, was perfect to work alongside my now 4-year-old and my newborn baby girl. I worked whilst she slept and absolutely loved the fact that when my son started school three months later, I could be there fully for them both.

The freedom and flexibility of being self-employed enabled me to earn whilst being around for all my children's milestones. I was there for their first day at school, sick days, sports days, appointments, etc. I just couldn't have a boss refusing leave to enable me to attend my child's assembly or making me feel guilty when they were sick. I felt like I had the best of both worlds, and I was extremely grateful. I continued to climb the career plan, and was earning my place on incentive trips, winning awards at conferences, and absolutely loving helping others earn money around their family life.

"The Universe has no choice but to bring you the direct manifestation of your thought about it." Neale Donald Walsh

Whilst at an annual conference, we had a presentation from inspirational speaker, Brian Mayne. Life has its pivotal moments, and this presentation became a catalyst to my learning journey into the mind, the laws of the universe, manifestation, and the world of quantum physics. If only they taught this stuff in school!

I had always been a positive, optimistic person and, like everyone else, had heard the quote, 'Whether you think you can or you think you can't, you're right', by Henry Ford. However, Brian didn't just say this quote, he explained the science behind it. When we have a positive thought, it triggers a chemical called serotonin. Of course, this is the chemical that gives us the feeling of happiness, but it also acts as a conductor, allowing connections within our brain and creating a 'train of thought'. In contrast, a negative thought triggers cortisone, which can make us feel low, sad, and depressed, effectively blocking the flow of thought or the 'thought train'. Of course, living this way long term can also have negative effects on our health too. This was the first time I had ever heard the science behind our thoughts, and I found it fascinating!

Whether we realise it or not, whether negative or positive, we are creating our own path in life.

I became a sponge to everything I could learn about our conscious and subconscious mind, and since this conference, I have read/listened to around 100 books!

Your subconscious will follow your lead. What you think about you 'subconsciously create'. Have you considered your thoughts before? Do you focus on where you want to be or dwell on the fact that you are not there yet?

When you think more positively, you notice those 'connections' within the brain, and you start to see solutions and new ideas 'spring' to mind. When opportunity comes your way, you actually see it, whereas people with a negative mindset don't even realise it presented itself and continue to complain. I remember a story Brian told us about a conversation he once had with a motorbike instructor. The instructor had told Brian about the number of incidents that motorbike drivers had with potholes in the road, and his advice to them was not to focus on the hole as subconsciously you drive yourself towards it. The key is to be aware of the hole, but don't stare at it—such a powerful lesson to carry in life.

Release what no longer serves you

With the arrival of Covid in 2020, times were uncertain. I was now home-schooling and adapting my business to the world we now lived in. I quickly realised that being a teacher wasn't for me, and my business was the one thing that kept me sane! However, I was extremely grateful that whilst many were facing uncertainty around their jobs and income, I could adapt and continue to earn whilst also being around my children, even if that did mean my new, luckily short-term, teacher role!

In 2021, the fire that had been burning inside of me for the business started to die out. I love learning, developing, and pushing myself, and I felt like my journey with my network marketing business had come to a natural end.

Finances had also taken a hit with the after-effects of covid, so I started to consider my options; I needed a new direction. But what!? I had been my own boss for so long, and I had got used to the flexibility of working when I chose, taking holidays when I decided, and was around for my kids. What could I possibly do that could give me all of that!?

After scouring the internet, I started to read about being a Virtual Assistant. That's it! Being a super organised person with experience in admin/PA roles and many years of experience working in the online space, developing and training a team, this was right up my street! Again, I threw myself in, spent hours reading as much as I could and soaking up as many YouTube videos and webinars as I could find. Soon after, I was ready to announce my new business venture!

Did I know exactly what I was doing? Nope! Of course, I had the experience, but doing it as a business was something different. I took action anyway, with the attitude of 'progress over perfection'.

The thing is, we can get wrapped up trying to be perfect before we start something new, but this can be us subconsciously procrastinating. Maybe we are just scared to start, that voice tells us that we are not good enough, so we 'just need to get this thing perfect first'. Like the quote from Martin Luther King says, 'You don't have to see the whole staircase, just take the first step.'

Remember, there are people less qualified and experienced than you, further ahead than you, because they took that first step. Courage will get you further than any perfect action.

You don't need to have everything figured out; I didn't have a website when I started, and I designed my own logo on Canva—progress over perfection. With this attitude, I announced my new business on social media and soon picked up my first clients! It seemed that there was a need for virtual business support. This is totally understandable, running a business requires you to juggle a lot of balls. The busier you get, the more balls you need to juggle, and eventually, some balls start to get dropped! Plus, let's face it, some balls are just not as much fun as others!

I was working the two businesses alongside each other, but something still didn't feel right. The energy and passion for my network marketing business just wasn't there anymore. I had tried to ignore it, but being a big believer in instinct and universal signs, I decided to ask for just that, a sign from the universe to tell me what I should do, and it was received the very next day! I walked into a supermarket, picked up a book off the shelf (Manifest Dive Deeper), flicked through and landed on a page with this quote in capital letters, 'ACCEPTING THAT SOMETHING ISN'T WORKING IS NOT A FAILURE – IT IS A POWER MOVE. IT IS A RELEASE OF WHAT NO LONGER SERVES YOU AND AN UNLOCKING OF A NEW BEGINNING.'

Well, I asked, I received, and I listened, so I walked away from that business with nothing but happiness and gratitude for what it had given me over the years, not only in income and time with my children but also in friendships, empowerment, incentive trips, experiences, and self-development.

As the statement in the book said, 'It is a release of what no longer serves you, and an unlocking of a new beginning'. It was exactly that for me. My VA business really started to build, and more opportunities started to come my way. It really was like I had removed what no longer served me to make room for the new. Don't you just love the magic of the universe?!

I have always been in tune with and followed my gut instinct, apart from one occasion when I took a PA role. During the interview, I got a bad vibe from one of the interviewees. This was not the person that I would be working with, so I ignored my gut, which told me to refuse the job offer, and accepted the role. What a huge mistake that was. Yep, my gut was right, this person was horrible, and a few months later, I walked out with no job to go to. That day, I made a promise to myself to NEVER go against my gut ever again.

'I'm not messing around here.'

These were the exact words I said to my husband once the path had been cleared to go all in with my Virtual Assistant business. I felt as though I had learnt as much as I possibly could on my own. It was time to hire a coach! That first year in business was my most difficult year financially. At one point, I was in tears to my husband, feeling like a failure as what I was contributing to the household finances wasn't what it had been previously, and I was feeling the pressure. I knew that I could make this business work. I had faith in myself, and I was committed to building a successful business. So, whilst this was the most difficult year financially, it was the year I invested the most. I had a vision, and I knew where I wanted to take my business. But I also knew that I couldn't get there as quickly as I wanted to alone. In the coming months, I had a session with a VA coach, worked with a sales and strategy coach and joined a membership for entrepreneurs.

I believe that surrounding yourself with the right people is crucial. People who will lift you up, people who are already where you want to be, people that are also determined to grow and develop. When you are self-employed, it can be lonely, so when you surround yourself with people like this, it is powerful and key to continuous growth.

My business was now really starting to grow, and my capacity was running out, so as I had loved developing a team with my last business, I decided to start to grow a team with my VA business too.

When I put out my first advert to take on associate VAs, I soon had over 70 applications. The common theme was mums, just like me, with great experience and expertise, who craved both income and time with their children. They didn't want to have to choose one or the other! And why should they? One said that she had recently returned to work after having her third child and only had £1 left after paying childcare fees!

Life & Motherhood coach Charlie Brown talks about how when we become a mother, we split in two; we are both woman and mother. The woman may want to push her career/business, but the mother may pile on the guilt. On the other hand, the mother may want to be at home with the children, but the woman worries about how that will affect her career/business, which, again, leads to more guilt!

More and more mums are looking to leave the corporate world, to find a more flexible way to be around for the kids but still earn money without the guilt the employment world can bring. This is why I am so passionate about helping women, especially mums; there is a way to have both.

I finally finished working through the applications, and at 1 am one night/morning, I went to bed, woke my husband up, and said, 'I can help these women'. So, not only did I start to take on my first team members to help me with the growing workload, I began to create my course to help others set up and scale their own VA business.

Helping others grow, develop and gain confidence was a huge part of my previous business and what I enjoyed the most. I was approached by the incredible coach, Emma Cooper, owner of Entrepreneursity, the membership that I was a part of. She not only wanted me to become the Virtual Assistant expert for the community but also wanted to team up to help people become certified Virtual Assistants! So, my course passed rigorous checks, became CPD Accredited, launched inside of The Certification Academy, Emma's other business, and I became the Certification Tutor.

This is what I love! Throughout all my coaching, from the years within my previous business to my VA business, I see so many women with goals and dreams, and they are perfectly capable of achieving them, but they just don't believe in themselves. So, helping people gain clarity, direction, and that all-important self-belief, really does light me up! Watching people grow and achieve what they want to achieve is even better than achieving it yourself!

"What if I fall? Oh, but my darling, what if you fly?"
Erin Hanson

Setting up, running, and growing your own business is no walk in the park. There are times you doubt yourself, allowing 'little miss imposter syndrome' to chirp up and convince you that everyone else is so much better than you! You struggle with the comfort zone battle, knowing that you need to get out of that safety zone, but it just feels so uncomfortable! You fear what others will think and say about you. You question if you are good enough and compare yourself to others who are much further ahead than you. You sacrifice time, energy, and sleep!

I believe that the most important thing you need to focus on to make any business succeed is mindset. If you are committed to showing up, have determination to learn, take action and keep going even when times feel hard, you will succeed.

You must be willing to ride the rollercoaster. There will be highs, and there will be lows. I decided to have a 'word of the year' for each year in my business. I find that this one word helps to set the tone for the year and is like an invisible compass. My current word is 'Expand'. I plan to have a picture made at some point with each year and the word to put up on my wall.

Some things I have learnt along my journey.

What other people think of you is none of your business – we can get eaten up worrying about what other people think of us. However, we all see the world through a different lens, we have different opinions and thoughts, and let's face it, some people are just not feeling great about the world, so they have negative opinions. This is none of our business. There are billions of people on this planet, they won't all like you, and you won't like all of them either! You are not everyone's cup of tea, and that is ok! Get over it and keep moving!

Comparison is the thief of joy – we all do it, we look at other people and start to compare ourselves. Looking around at what other people in our industry are doing is great, we can take inspiration, but try not to compare yourself. They might have been in business for years, whilst you may just be starting out. It really doesn't make any sense to compare, does it? Don't let your ice cream melt whilst counting someone else's sprinkles!

Be aware of what you consume – I am not talking about diet here; we all love a bit of chocolate cake, don't we?! I am talking about mentally, what TV programmes do you watch? What books do you read? What podcasts do you listen to? Do you watch the news, then feel sad and scared about the world that we live in? What do you consume from the people around you? Do you spend time with positive people or energy drainers? Become aware of what you are mentally consuming.

Don't dwell on the opinions of people who haven't achieved what you want to achieve – it really doesn't matter if Suzy down the street thinks that your business idea is silly, or that her friends, cousins, aunty tried the same idea, and it was a flop! Try to only take advice seriously from those who have been on a similar journey to you or are where you want to be, and even then, take it as just that, advice. This is your path and your journey.

Stretch your comfort zone – take baby steps if you need to, but get comfortable with being uncomfortable. It may be that you hate posting selfies (me too!) but know that you need to be visible to grow your business, so start getting used to posting a picture of yourself. Over time, that circle of comfort zone expands, and what you once saw as something you would NEVER do, you are now willing to do! For example, when I was at the start of my network marketing business, my upline asked me to deliver some training at our monthly session. I flat-out refused! However, over time my confidence grew, and I went from flat-out refusing, to delivering a session to a small room, to planning and leading regular sessions, to delivering a session to a room of hundreds and speaking in online communities of thousands. This was a gradual process. You need to expand your comfort zone circle gradually.

Energy Flows where attention goes – be aware of what you are giving your attention to. Is it the focus and desire to get to where you want to be, or is it on all the reasons why you haven't achieved it yet? We get more of what we focus on.

Perfection doesn't exist – stop waiting for things to be perfect—progress over perfection.

Set boundaries – know what you will and will not accept in life and in business and stick to those boundaries.

Fall Forward – when you hit hurdles in your business, or something doesn't go as planned, learn the lesson, adapt and improve. Have you watched the university graduation speech from Denzel Washington? I recommend it if not! You don't fail when you fall, you fail when you refuse to get up - don't see failure as failure – see it as learning.

Ask for help and support when you need it – asking for help is not a sign of weakness, it is knowing your limits and being self-aware. Many people run into burnout because they felt that they could, or should, do it all alone. Don't let yourself get to that point. It might be simply asking for advice, collaborating, or delegating tasks.

Get out of your own way – the only thing that will stop you from succeeding is YOU! Everyone is on a different journey to what they see as success. Some will get there quickly, and others will get there more slowly. But one thing is for sure, you absolutely won't get there if you stop! So, get out of your own way.

"The only thing standing between you and your goal is the bullshit story you keep telling yourself as to why you can't achieve it." Jordan Belfort

More than just Admin Support

With a rise in people leaving the corporate world and seeking flexible income, more people are looking to become or work with a Virtual Assistant. However, there are still lots of people who don't know that flexible freelance support even exists! A Virtual Assistant is like your business wing woman (or man). My business supports entrepreneurs and CEOs with flexible business support. This could be managing emails, social media support, or supporting a client with the wide range of tasks that comes with launching a new offer or service. It is very varied!

I quickly recognised that many of my clients struggled with time management and also liked having someone to hold them accountable, so I introduced my stand-alone Time Management strategy sessions and Accountability packages. Some people just need that gentle nudge or a good kick up the bum!

Here is my statement about what being a Virtual Assistant means to me. 'Being a Virtual Assistant is much more than offering admin support, it is being a wing woman, someone who takes on your dreams and goals and who is just as determined as you to achieve them. It is being someone to encourage you when that self-doubt voice chirps up and someone to run ideas over. Someone to hold you accountable and to be on your business journey with you.'

THE RISE OF THE FEMALE ENTREPRENEUR

What does your current or future business mean to you? What is your mission statement? Writing this out is a great exercise to cement your values and the impact you wish to make.

My business journey is ever-evolving. I love to learn, develop, and keep moving forwards. I like spotting areas of opportunity to improve myself and my business, and I have lots of exciting plans. Who knows where it will evolve in the future? Will I get that land and rescue animals? Who knows ...

Wherever you are in your journey, I wish you all the success in the world.

If you would like to connect with me, I would love to hear from you! Feel free to drop me an email or find me on social media. You can find all my links, including my free eBooks, within my Linktr.ee below.

LinkTree: https://linktr.ee/gemmahowarthva

"It ain't about how hard you hit, it's about how hard you can get hit and keep moving forward, how much you can take and keep moving forward. That's how winning is done."
Rocky Balboa

CHAPTER 11
Jenna Richardson
Chief Energy Officer

Made for More – A Momprenuer's Passionate and Purposeful Pursuit for Paradigm Shift

Chaos and Questions

You know that moment where you realize that perhaps everything you are isn't really you at all?

I remember mine. I was sitting in the parking lot of a Home Depot store with my sleeping infant in his car seat. Why was I in the Home Depot parking lot? No idea. I didn't need anything. I didn't even enter the store. I was just sitting, crying, contemplating, and complaining to a friend over the phone about how extremely lost I was feeling. Now, I don't believe that this was postpartum, but who knows? There could have been a hint of that. What I do know is that I was feeling 100%, completely unaligned with how I had been living my life up until that point.

I was 36 years old, a first-time mom, a new wife, and a successful strategic sales executive working in international business. I had known that motherhood would change my life significantly, but I was expecting that to be the extrinsic stuff. No more jet setting off to London or Paris or quick stops in Ibiza on my way to Monte Carlo. No more late-night networking in New York City or champagne-centered business lunches, and I was cool with that. I had done all the things, and honestly, I was over it.

But I had no idea how much it would change me intrinsically. For a while, even before the birth of Carter, I had felt unsure and uneasy about where my career had taken me. But what I wasn't expecting was the deep, dare I say, despair that I was feeling in that moment. The uncertainty. The confusion. The emptiness. The feeling that everything that I had done, everything that I had been, everything I had worked for, achieved, accomplished, identified with, that it wasn't really me, that it had never been me. But, even deeper than that, if that wasn't me, then who the hell was I?

And in that moment, amidst my bantering and blubbering, my beautiful friend, Jessica, said something to me that would change the trajectory of my life. It was one simple sentence—three simple words. But the impact that they had that day, and every day thereafter, literally changed my life. I had met Jessica at a women's networking event in Hoboken, NJ. We were both crazy type A overachievers, both in our mid-30s, both getting married in the coming year, and both with big corporate jobs, big personalities, and big mouths, and we hit it off instantly. We had since left "the city" and relocated to different parts of New Jersey, but we had stayed in touch, and we were the type of friends that no matter where we were in life, no matter how long it had been since we had spoken, if we were in trouble, in distress, in despair, we were only a phone call or text message away.

When I met Jess, she had just left her corporate job in the pharmaceutical industry and had embarked on a whole new personal and professional journey, going back to school to become an Integrative Health and Nutrition Coach. When she had initially shared this with me, I was intrigued.

I come from a medical family, my father is a Medical Doctor, and my mom a Registered Nurse, and coming from a small town in upstate New York and having a strong propensity for math and science, it was always assumed that I would become a doctor. Well, those dreams were quickly shattered when I went off to Cornell University and realized very quickly that I couldn't stand the sight of blood or the smell of formaldehyde, and I got a D- in Chem 101. So, I made a quick shift and graduated with a degree in business communications.

But I do believe that helping and healing is in my DNA, and I had always been interested in health and fitness, so this health coach thing sounded interesting. What was a health coach anyway?

Clarity through Action

I immediately drove the 10 minutes home that rainy weekday afternoon, following my chat with Jess, and hopped on my computer. Within minutes, I had enrolled in the yearlong program with the Institute for Integrative Nutrition to become a Certified Integrative Health and Nutrition Coach.

Now I didn't leave my corporate job right away. I was on maternity leave for a bit and working for a London-based company, working from home, and fitting my studies in around my day job, caring for an infant, and all the other new mom stuff. But I was LIT UP. I would get up in the wee hours of the morning to listen to the modules, feverishly scribbling notes at the dining room table. I would take Carter on long walks around the neighborhood, headphones in, absorbing all the content I could. I was learning so many amazing things about farming, food and fulfillment, and I felt ALL OF IT. I had found my calling, my "thing", my SELF in this content, course, and potential new career. I was elated.

During this time, my mom had been traveling back and forth from upstate NY to NJ to help me care for Carter while I worked, studied and traveled. My Dad would come down on the weekends to visit after a long week in the busy conglomerate-owned medical practice that he led, and they could see and feel the passion that I had for this new path. I mean, how could they not? I couldn't keep my mouth shut about our food, our water, and our air. I had started visiting the farmers market on a weekly basis, trading take out for home cooked meals. I was making baby food for God's sake.

My father, always curious and open to new ideas, became intrigued and decided to explore this newly found concept, which we were terming "functional medicine". He enrolled at the Institute for Functional Medicine to do their foundational intro intensive, and the words that he spoke to me upon returning from that event are literally etched in my brain and cause goose bumps to form whenever I share them. When I asked how he had enjoyed the training, he said to me, "After practicing medicine for more than 30 years, I finally feel like I have the tools to help people get well and not just keep them sick". Chills.

Little did I know how valuable, life-changing and life-saving this new information, insight, and intelligence would be for my family and so many other amazing people.

When Carter was six months old, he started to display some strange health-related symptoms. He developed a sporadic head tilt that was "diagnosed" as torticollis, he fell off the growth chart, and he was having digestive and motility challenges. Our pediatrician referred us to a physical therapist who helped temporarily, but within a week, his symptoms returned. At my prompting, she also referred us to a pediatric gastroenterologist, who looked at me as if I had ten heads when I explained that I believed the head tilt to be related to his digestive challenges.

Doctor after doctor, therapist after therapist, and no answers. We finally ended up in the office of a young and more progressive pediatric GI who heard what I had to say and agreed that perhaps his symptoms could all be related. He prescribed a PPI medication to help with digestive discomfort. I gave Carter the medication later that evening, and slowly over the next few days he completely stopped eating; he wouldn't even nurse.

In my first-time mom panic, I called the doctor's office on Monday morning. I spoke with the young doctor who told me, "Don't worry, I'll simply call in another prescription which will stimulate his appetite." Again, I returned to the pharmacy, and to this day, I have so much gratitude for the pharmacist on duty, the one that caught the error that could have been catastrophic for my family.

This pharmacist, on that morning, called me over to the consultation area and asked, how old is your son? Is the date on this prescription correct?".

I replied that it was correct, Carter was six months old, and his exact words that followed still cause me to shutter, "You know that this medication is severely contraindicated for children under the age of two, he could stop breathing and die." In that moment I think I almost died, blacked out, saw red, however you want to describe it. I was a mess of emotions, enraged, hopeless, terrified, and appalled. All. The. Things.

Root Cause Renegade

Now, I knew that the healthcare system in the US was broken. I watched my father deal with it every day. Out of the house before the sun came up. Churning through patients to meet "productivity goals". Charting well into the evening because normal working hours didn't allow for admin time. But, up until that point, I was more of an observer of the dysfunction. Now, it was personal.

I composed myself that morning, went home, and hopped on my laptop. I was determined to accomplish two key things: figure out what was going on with my infant son and fix the broken system that we know as healthcare (sick care).

With a background in management consulting, where the main function is finding the root cause of operational dysfunction in business, my question was, WHY? Why is this happening? Why was no doctor looking for the root cause of what was going on with my son? Why was the system so quick to throw medication at a baby, and one that could potentially cause harm? It was baffling to me.

All this was occurring around the time that I sat in the Home Depot parking lot. Coincidence, I think not. What I know and accept in the depths of my soul, almost a decade later, is that everything happens for a reason. We are all on a path. We are all on this earth to do something, create something, contribute something. And, in the midst of the chaos of this time, I knew that I had found my purpose, my passion, and so much amazing potential to create change that would impact the lives of many.

Now the feeling that I was "made for more" didn't happen overnight. Though I have to admit, I do remember that feeling in the pit of my stomach and in my soul, even as an adolescent. When asked why I wanted to be a doctor at my high school graduation, my response was that I wanted to find the cure for cancer. So, big dreams, yes. My Gen X generation of women were the first that were positioned to be it all, have it all, do it all, so I always had desire, drive, and determination.

But I don't know that I had the confidence or even the consciousness, and I certainly didn't have the passion that came from the highly personal and purposeful mission that I found, or that found me, in this turn of events. I also didn't understand the power of choice and the magic of creation, nor the connection between these two things. That didn't come until much later for me, when I dove into the power of the mind and the laws of the universe, quantum physics, and all that cool and nerdy stuff.

Completely disenchanted with the conventional medical system and model, and with my father on-board with this "new age" way of practicing, I knew exactly what was next. We needed to create a clinic, an environment, where others struggling with the chaos of the system, where others seeking answers, solutions, and root cause resolution could come to be heard, to be seen, to be understood, and to be helped and healed. No more revolving door of doctors, no more pill for every ill, no more laundry list of "ologists". It was time for a true paradigm shift, and thus was born Princeton Integrative Health (PIH).

Trapped By Trauma

The clinic grew organically, through word-of-mouth, because we were different, because we listened, because we cared, because we helped folks to regain their health, regain their life, regain their self. It was beautiful and rewarding work, but it was slow. And there were days when doubt and challenges crept in. Staff conflicts, changes, chaos, and then the big one, COVID, which shut down our in-person patient care for months. And yet we stayed the course and were there to pick up the pieces on the other side of the pandemic.

We bounced back from Covid, and as much of a curse as it was, it was also a blessing. It forced folks to wake up and start to pay better attention to their health. It was also a time for deep personal work for me. Up to that point, I had been so focused on the physical and physiologic elements of health. But what I realized through the pandemic was just how much both emotions and energetics impact health and well-being.

I looked back on the hundreds of patients we had seen and began to assess the success stories and the struggles. I had my philosophy that the root cause of disease and dysfunction always went back to three things: deficiency, toxicity, and trauma. We had gotten good at addressing the first two, but we didn't have a great solution for the last, and post-pandemic, everyone had trauma.

I began to conceptualize a new model for health, with physical health at the foundation, because if you don't have that, you have nothing. On top of that, physiologic health, meaning balance and function, then emotional health, and at the top, energetic health, meaning our state of being or how we show up in the world.

I also took a hard look at myself. I had spent a good portion of those two years at home with my family. Two young kids, ages six and two at the time, navigating online learning for my son, keeping my daughter entertained and occupied, and my husband and I both trying to work from home. It was tough. It's often in the hard times that we see our true selves, and early in the pandemic, I didn't like what I saw. I was angry, irritated, frustrated, and unavailable emotionally for my family. So focused on the bad and totally blind to the beauty of the situation. My emotional and energetic health was way out of whack.

I was introspective. If I was showing up this way at home, for my family, for the tiny humans whom I cared for more than anything in the world, how was I showing up for my practice, for our patients, and for our staff? It was not the leadership that I knew. Now, what to do about it. I knew that these challenges for me were deeply rooted. I'd had my own trauma which caused me to be distant, reactive, always on edge, confrontational and even aggressive at times, a "cold bitch" as a friend once called me (again, thank you, Jessica). Now to get to the root and resolve it.

As always, I sought solutions through education. I had trauma on my mind, both for supporting our patients and because I knew that it was the root of what was holding me back in life, in relationships, in business, and from being my best self.

I had been in therapy on and off for many years. But what I found about the conventional approach of talk therapy is that it was similar to the challenges in health care; it kept me stuck in my stories, rehashing my issues, never moving forward. It was just like a prescription for a disease, masking the symptoms, never resolving the root cause.

Now, I get that we can't undo trauma. It's in the past, it's contributed to who we are, but we can make a choice in how it defines us. I began to explore more unconventional methods of therapy, EMDR, DNRS, hypnotherapy, etc. I became intrigued by hypnotherapy and was days away from starting a hypnotherapy training program when I found something even more magical: Rapid Transformational Therapy ® (RTT).

From Calling to Creation

RTT® is a therapeutic approach that combines hypnotherapy with neuro-linguistic programing (NLP), cognitive behavioral therapy (CBT), psychotherapy, and neuroscience to help clients uncover the root cause of challenges to bust through belief systems (BS), transform triggers and create a life they love.

I started the RTT® program in November and ate up the content. It was the piece that I, that we, had been missing. The subconscious belief systems keeping us stuck, the stories that we replay over and over again about not being enough, not being safe, not being capable, not being worthy. The root of the issues that so many of us face in seeking health, happiness, and harmony.

I spent an entire week in California in an RTT® intensive, and the things that I learned about others and about myself, but more importantly, the things that I let go and released literally changed my life. I knew that this was a practice that I needed to bring to PIH and beyond. Coupled with the fundamentals of nervous system regulation, another modality that I love and leverage, RTT® has been a game-changer for me and for my clients/patients. I believe this is a fundamental part of the future of healthcare. The emotional and energetic piece is rarely assessed or addressed in the current environment, but it's such an integral component to overall health and well-being.

Today, I use RTT® in practice, both in the clinic as well as with private clients. I work with people, mostly women, who are seeking to get out of their own way and out of their own stories to stop the vicious cycle of self-sabotage and self-doubt, and to step into their power.

From this work, I have created a coaching and educational platform that I call One Rich Life. One Rich Life is about achieving ultimate fulfillment in every dimension. It's not just about financial prosperity, but rather a comprehensive, holistic richness that encompasses health, relationships, career, and more. It's about living your life as the YOU that you desire and deserve to be, about breaking free from limiting beliefs and expectations and identities that once defined you but no longer serve you, and embracing change to create a life that is in alignment with your true authentic self and amazing aspirations.

To me, this is true wellness or, as I call it, "wellth". It's not just the absence of disease or dysfunction, but it's about making choices, taking control, creating clarity, and developing the courage and confidence to step out of your comfort zone and take chances that will literally change your life.

In the depths of my journey, what I realize is that this was my true lesson. From the confused chaos that I felt in that Home Depot parking lot to an entirely new cause, career, platform, and more, I am a living example that you truly can rise up from the depths of despair to create a life that you LIVE (because how many of us aren't truly living, but just existing), a life that you LOVE, and a life that creates a lasting impact and, eventually, leaves a LEGACY.

So, if you are feeling lost, uncertain, or unaligned, take it as a signal, a sign. Take action. Trust yourself. Trust the process. Define your dreams. Feel that burning desire to seek answers or shift a paradigm.

- **Make the choice.**
- **Take the chance.**
- **Create the change.**

Start with you. Because ultimately, it's up to you. Your One Rich Life awaits you. Step into that life, one lived with purpose, passion, and potential, where every day feels meaningful, joyful, and rewarding. You have the power. You are made for more.

To learn more about my work or to connect with me, please visit LinkTree: https://linktr.ee/onerichlife.

CHAPTER 12
Joanna Oakley
Argylestone Consulting Ltd

Change to Transformation

I have been in the recruitment and staffing industry for over 20 years, working for some of the leading and most recognised names globally within the sector. Over the years, I steadily worked my way through the businesses until eventually reaching the level of Board Director in 2018. I spent 4+ years as COO for the UK arm of a global recruitment business, one which at the time held fourth place within the global staffing rankings. In 2022, I changed direction and decided to set up my own limited company, Argylestone

Consulting, providing change and transformation consultancy back into the staffing industry.

Like many, I fell into recruitment, but what keeps me here is my desire to find strategies to avoid complacency, drive continuous improvement and help staffing businesses innovate their recruitment processes, allowing them to add real value to their candidates and clients and remove unnecessary cost from their businesses.

Whether it's the recruiters themselves or recruitment organisations, I see many who get stuck in a rut with contentment for the status quo and doing things the way they have always done them, many of which are still relying on manual processes and ways of working.

I remember Greg Savage (author and recruitment industry expert) telling a story about a recruiter who boasted ten years of experience, to which Greg replied, "You don't have ten years of experience; you have one year of experience done ten times over, you're no better now than you were after 12 months" and the reason for it, he went on to explain, was that the recruiter closed his mind to learning. It's the same with recruitment businesses, so often I hear of recruitment organisations who have invested huge sums of money in updating their recruitment systems, only to re-engineer the workflows within it, to fit their 10-15-year-old processes and ways of working, which makes them less efficient and productive than they were beforehand.

I am often asked by career-minded recruiters looking to get into leadership roles how, as a female, I gained the experience needed to create a successful leadership role while maintaining a work-life balance.

For me, I work no more or no less than I want to. For the most part, I love work, I always have, so putting in maximum effort wasn't ever really a chore. I also recognise that I have made decisions in my life which has allowed me to focus solely on my career. The biggest of these decisions was not to have kids, but it wasn't always that way.

How did I get here?

Looking back, I would describe my own early childhood as ordinary. By the age of 8, my parents divorced, and my mother, brother and I moved away. From there things became more difficult. I wasn't bothered by the divorce as such, as my mother made everything "an exciting adventure", but I am not going to lie, there were some awful times. As some wise person once said to me, "Life isn't supposed to be easy if it is, you're doing it wrong, every obstacle is a lesson to learn from". That quote has stuck with me.

Having had a real love for first school, I was disappointed to discover that big school was not as fun. I eventually found myself in a catholic convent school run by nuns, and there I found my happy place. The structure and discipline (not that I was a rule follower by any stretch) I was frequently in trouble, but I loved the nuns. After a couple of years, the school amalgamated with the catholic boy's school next door, and I lost interest. I was never particularly academic, though I did do well in Religious Education and, surprisingly, business studies.

I was bullied in secondary school which also dampened my enjoyment. Frequently getting beaten up by an older boy at my school when I stepped off the bus. Never quite sure why. Eventually, I told my parents, and my dad resolved the matter. We eventually moved house, and not long after, the bullying started again, but this time from a girl who lived down my road who was just plain nasty. By the time school finished, I couldn't wait to get into work. I knew at an early age I loved travel, and with my dad working in the airline industry for many years, I was keen to do the same.

If there were any opportunities for work experience at the airport, I was there. School holidays etc, I worked my way around British Airways departments gaining as much experience and understanding as I could. I didn't care that I wasn't paid; I was happy to get up at 3.30 am for a 4.30 start and I learnt a huge amount during that time. After college I landed my first proper airline role.

Early in my airport career, I hit a dark time that stayed with me for years. It wasn't one specific incident but a series of events that left me feeling overwhelmed and disconnected from others. My health suffered, relationships failed, and I became afraid of commitment. Even owning pets was difficult for me. Meanwhile, friends and family seemed to be thriving, while I felt lost and without direction. After five years in the airline industry, low wages forced me to seek a customer service job in IT, which led me to become a Customer Services Executive at a major laptop manufacturer.

In the 90s, the IT and telecoms industry was not ideal, and I faced multiple redundancies. In 2003, I joined recruitment at a well-known staffing brand, recommended by my best friend, Charlotte. Despite no experience, my track record in sales spoke for itself. I became a branch manager and quickly turned around our "Dog branches." Later, I joined a great team in Welwyn with supportive managers, and we saw growth in performance. After five years, I followed one of our directors to a new brand, to a staffing firm. Back in 2006, they were only known for their flex staff, and I was offered the opportunity to join their business as a branch manager at their branch down the road from their head office. If I remember rightly, they were having their first branch IT system installed the week I arrived, so they were making the transition from application cards to the computer!!

Again, I found myself within a team of incredible managers and an amazing boss. My performance at work was great, I had several years overachieving on budgets, my staff were winning accolades left, right and centre, and I couldn't have been happier for them. Personally, however, my life had started to unravel. I was literally held together by work and the incredible team of people I had around me, from my boss, my fellow branch managers, and people in my team. I can't pinpoint what it was specifically that started to turn the tide, but what I can say is I really started to pay attention to other people who, for some reason completely unbeknown to me, seemed to refuse to let me fail.

My nan Julia was one of those people. In her late 90s, the woman was a rock; I spoke to her weekly and visited monthly or whenever I was in London, and her subtle words of wisdom and gentle questioning have left a mark to this day. My friend Laura was another. I never understood quite what I did to deserve such a gift, but even now, I doubt she fully understands quite how grateful I am to her. By the time I hit my late 30s, things were improving, and I started to really work on myself. It's funny when you eventually reach the age you first remember your mother being when you were a child and realise how quite not ready for being an adult you really are.

For me, that age was 32. I had not always appreciated my mother, like many of us, I am sure, and I certainly had no concept as to what it meant to be a single parent on one income trying to hold down a full-time job with two nightmare kids at home. At the time, it didn't register that my mother's fondness for an apple and a slice of cheese wasn't because of her love for the healthy snack but because we didn't have the money, and she focused on feeding us rather than herself.

Our family went through some tough times, but looking back, there were still moments of joy and excitement. Despite any financial struggles, our mum always found a way to make things special for us kids. One of our favourite activities was riding on the hood of her Nissan Micra in the parking lot of our flats. She would hit the brakes suddenly just to shake us off, and we thought it was the most thrilling adventure. Our mum was also fierce and protective; I'll never forget the time she saw some older boys trying to steal our bikes. At only 5ft 1", she drove her car over to their place and fearlessly confronted them. I couldn't have been prouder.

In my late thirties, I met my now husband. We dated for a year before I was introduced to his two children. I must admit, I was afraid. The idea of becoming a stepparent was daunting, especially since I had no desire for children of my own. I also didn't want to be in a relationship where I always came last, and the thought of dealing with an ex-wife didn't exactly thrill me. My divorce had taught me how easy it is to lose yourself in a relationship, and I made sure not to make the same mistake again. As time passed, I began to understand what I truly wanted and did not want in life and what was important to me.

I continued to work hard, and though it was challenging at times, I received internal job offers and moved between divisions within the staffing business. Over the years, I had the opportunity to work with incredibly talented individuals and learn from some of the best in the industry. As my career progressed, my personal life started to fall into place as well. I rediscovered my love for learning and pursued various courses and qualifications that supported my exciting career.

Overcoming Inadequacy - Who are you?

I'll be honest: not attending university made me feel inadequate for a long time. There were moments when I let others make me feel foolish and unintelligent. But as I reflect on my portfolio of achievements and credentials, I know that I am far from being stupid. I also acknowledge that everyone has their own unique style of learning, and this is an area where schools could improve. In the past, I struggled in school due to the teaching methods used, but now I have no trouble learning at my own pace.

In my 40s, my career was thriving, and my home life was finally stable. I felt like I was truly living my best life. However, there was a point where I was at risk of being let go due to a company restructure. Thankfully, I was offered an internal position, which may have seemed like a demotion on paper with lower pay and fewer benefits, but I saw it as an adventure and didn't want to leave the company. Working onsite with clients was new for me, and as my mother would say, it was "an adventure." And it was! Of course, it wasn't without its challenges; my team and I were pulling long hours just to keep our heads above water. During this time, my colleague and friend Sue pulled me aside one day and gently said, "Everyone hates you. You may be great at your job, but if you don't start showing a softer side (which I know you have), your staff will all leave."

I strongly believe that everything happens for a reason in life, and people come into your life when you need them the most. Despite the challenges I faced in the first few years, I consider myself truly blessed. It wasn't until then that I realised how disconnected I had become from other people. Small talk was unbearable for me; I just couldn't do it. I struggled to relate to others, avoided physical contact, and constantly felt afraid. Afraid that my facade of having everything under control would be shattered, revealing the scared little kid inside. I was also very lonely as a result.

Back then, I didn't have a label for it, but now I know that what I experienced was imposter syndrome. Above all else, I was drained of energy. Trying to appear put-together and confident took its toll on me, leaving me exhausted. No matter what challenges came my way - health problems, family issues, job instability - I refused to let them shake me.

Enough: A Moment of Self-Acceptance

It was the 10th of August. I don't remember the day, but I decided enough was enough. It was genuinely like a lightbulb moment when I decided I just wasn't going to care what anyone else thought of me, and I just needed to be me, and that started with self-care. I stopped drinking and smoking, and I began to exercise more. I started chatting to colleagues (granted I think initially they wondered what the hell was wrong with me), talking to strangers and making a daily list of everything I had to be grateful for.

I let go of others' expectations and opinions of me and instead focused on my own desires and boundaries. I learned to confidently say no without feeling the need to justify my decision. It was liberating to realise that I didn't always need a reason for saying no. So, the next time someone asks you to do something you're not keen on, try simply saying, "No, thank you." Most people will respect your decision without pressing for an explanation. And for those who do ask, it's okay to be honest and say, "I don't want to." It took some time, but eventually things started falling into place for me. I was promoted multiple times, and even took on a leadership role despite initially feeling underqualified. I realised there was nothing to lose and decided to take the chance. Yes, it was challenging at first and joining the leadership team wasn't easy, but my mentors and coaches were invaluable in helping me navigate through it all.

My first few meetings were unforgettable. I felt like I had to justify my presence or involvement by constantly saying, "In my experience" or "based on previous experience." Luckily, that feeling didn't last long. It wasn't the tasks that were challenging, but rather the expected behaviours. There was no manual for becoming a board director and not having to ask for permission to do certain things. Similarly, there was no preparation for transitioning from a senior leadership position to a seat on the board, where people would treat me differently or even resent my success. And this was not just limited to my male colleagues, if that's what you're thinking.

I stayed with this staffing business for almost ten years, and the last few years were the happiest of my career. I learnt so much during my time there, and for the first time, I can honestly say I made some lifelong friends. I was emotional the day I left. It had not always been the easiest time. We had by this point, been through several restructures, closed offices, opened a new HQ, and not everyone was able to continue the journey with us. Some decisions we made were tough to make, but like any leadership team, you must do what is best for the business, and that might not be what is best for the individual or even yourself.

If I could go home every night and look at myself in the mirror, knowing I had done my very best for people, that was all I could do. I am now very rapidly approaching 50, and my world looks so different. I still don't drink or smoke. My career has absolutely blossomed, I couldn't be happier. Working for myself has been an experience I never thought I would enjoy and certainly wasn't something I ever thought I would have the confidence to do.

My health has improved, and as I said to my mother, if I were to drop dead tomorrow, that would be OK because I am in a great place, and I feel so lucky and utterly blessed. On occasion, when I do open up about my past and my childhood, people often ask what I would change. My answer is absolutely nothing. There were many occasions where life sucked, and I mean truly appalling, while I absolutely would not want to repeat certain periods of my life, everything that happened, taught me something, even today, I always look to understand the lesson.

It might not be obvious, but it's there, and sometimes you can be in the hell, not for yourself, but to get someone else through it, you are someone else's gift. I recently read a Washington Post article; the author shares a moment of despair and suicidal thoughts. As the author prepares to take his life, a stranger interrupts him at a train platform, asking for his help to take a photo. Despite feeling lost, the author takes photos of the cheerful woman instead. This interaction saved the man's life.

I often wondered if the young woman knew she had saved someone's life. Maybe she didn't, and her own life was filled with struggles. Perhaps this trip was a chance for her to escape it all and have some fun, or maybe she lived an extraordinary life and was just on vacation - we will never know. I, too, have been fortunate enough to have many blessings come into my life at crucial moments. And while most of them may not realise it, they had a profound impact on me at that very moment.

I have so many people to be grateful for, people who have touched my life, good or bad, that I wouldn't be here without them. From managers and directors, peers and colleagues, and the incredible staff I have worked with over the years, watching them grow and forge amazing careers of their own has been a true highlight. I am also grateful to my stepdaughters, who have brought more joy into my life than I would have ever thought possible. I always wondered when I looked at my stepdad, how it was possible for a stranger to love my brother and me as if we were his own, and now, I understand.

As for the ex-wife, she's cool too, and I like her a lot. Like most things in life, blended families are not easy, but she and my husband created two amazing children whom I have been blessed with, and I am so lucky that together, we can share and enjoy all the kids' important milestones and occasions. I'd like to think that she knows if there was ever an issue, she could pick up the phone to me, and I'd be there.

People often ask me about the highlights of my career, and I am proud to say that one of them is being able to give others the same opportunities that were given to me. I believe in taking a chance on someone even if they may not have the exact education or experience but possess the right attitude and potential. It brings me great joy to see my clients' team members grow and develop their skills from the start to the end of a project. Even when they are no longer working with me, I am thrilled to see their successes and achievements on LinkedIn. Looking ahead, I am filled with excitement for what the future holds. My passion for this industry and its people drives me forward, not just money. I have the freedom to choose my clients and projects, as well as focus on things that truly matter to me, such as adding value and making a difference while having fun. Change can be difficult for people from all walks of life, so I understand that companies may feel anxious or worried when bringing in an external consultant like me. My goal is always to assist and support them in any way possible, rather than judge or criticise their work.

In my experience, actions carry more weight than words. When people work with me, they quickly realise that I don't care about past mistakes or imperfections; all that matters is the current task at hand and working together to accomplish it. Though I keep a gratitude journal every day, acknowledging the many blessings in my life, I also make sure to learn something new every single day. This constant pursuit of knowledge is crucial for continued growth and success. And over the past couple of years, I have built an incredible network of supportive women who lift me up, push me forward, and share many laughs with me - and I do the same for them.

I don't know everything, and let's face it, who does? I will always be a work in progress, but the point is to always try harder to be better. One of my greatest learnings is that life is tough, and happiness is a choice. We have many choices to make in life, and there are two decisions I try to make positively every day; one is to be happy, and the other is to be kind.

Embracing Change for Positive Impact

As we come to the end of this chapter, I urge you to join me on a journey towards professional and personal growth. Let's actively embrace change, prioritise actions over words, and work together towards achieving success. When choosing projects and clients, I make sure that our passions and values align, and I seek opportunities where I can make a meaningful impact. Consider how my skills and expertise could benefit your staffing organisation's success. If you think my abilities match your temporary staffing needs, I welcome further exploration. You can find me on LinkedIn or visit my website to see how we can collaborate for mutual success.

Joanna Oakley CCWP MCIPD | LinkedIn

Argylestone Consulting - Managed Service Programme, Change Management, Transformation, Change Management, Consulting, Managed Service Programme

THE RISE OF THE FEMALE ENTREPRENEUR

CHAPTER 13
Jessica Harvey
The Female Mentoring Alliance

Flight of Empowerment: From Risk-Averse to Alliance Founder

Embracing Uncertainty: A Leap Beyond Lists

"But what if I fall?" I squeaked from the precipice of Go Ape in Chessington, my heart pounding louder than the zip lines below. My husband, patient and composed, assured me with a comforting smile, "You have a harness and a hard hat on. You're completely safe; there's nothing to worry about."

Behind me stood my husband and son, my best friend, and her family, all eager to conquer the treetop adventure. Yet, paralysed by fear, I made a pivotal decision—I unclipped and settled underneath with a warm coffee, watching as others soared through the challenge I'd just deemed insurmountable.

As I sipped my coffee, a nagging thought lingered: What if I had embraced the fear? What if I had taken that leap? Would I have flown, and how would it have felt? This moment of hesitation would echo in my mind as I grappled with the unexpected turns that life would soon throw my way.

You see, I was the head girl at school, a compliance officer in a bank, and an unapologetic lover of rules. Certainty and control were my allies, and lists were my everything. Notice the past tense—I say "were" because the first thing that turned my world upside down was our beautiful son, Fynn.

Fynn, our IVF miracle, challenged everything. From those initial 4 cells to the enchanting gaze of his big blue eyes and chubby cheeks, he defied the order and predictability I so cherished. My meticulously crafted lists seemed irrelevant in the face of this tiny bundle of unpredictability. Fynn became the catalyst for a profound shift in perspective, teaching me that not everything needed to be perfect and that, beyond the facade of order and calm, there was more to life.

It was a lesson my laid-back husband had always appreciated. While I revelled in structure and planning, he found joy in spontaneity and the beauty of imperfection. Fynn, with his infectious laughter and unbridled curiosity, bridged the gap between our worlds, fostering a deeper understanding of the beauty that lies in embracing uncertainty.

As I sat beneath the treetops, watching others navigate the challenging course, I couldn't help but draw parallels to my own journey. The fear of the unknown and the apprehension of falling—these were not just sentiments reserved for the treetop adventure but reflections of my internal struggle to break free from the constraints of my own making.

In the following chapter, I will explore the moments when life demanded that I step outside my comfort zone, confront my fears, and embrace the unforeseen. From challenging the conventions of my career and what I thought I wanted, each experience became a stepping stone toward a more authentic and fulfilling life.

Join me as I navigate this adventure, not with a list in hand but with an open heart, ready to discover the richness that lies beyond the safety of the familiar. It's a journey of self-discovery, resilience, and the unwavering belief that sometimes, in letting go of the fear of falling, we find the exhilaration of soaring.

From Calculations to Compliance: Embracing Risks and Building a Career Brand

In the dynamic world of banking, where risk is often calculated, my journey took an unexpected turn. As someone naturally risk averse, I found myself on a path that diverged significantly from the conventional career trajectory. It was a journey marked by surprises, opportunities, and the invaluable support of my laid-back husband.

Initially set on becoming an accountant, my aspirations took a hit when I faced the harsh reality of exams and subsequent dismissal. This setback, however, led me to the role of a compliance officer, where I spent two decades navigating the intricate landscape of banking and ensuring adherence to regulations.

By the age of 40, I achieved the remarkable milestone of becoming a managing director in a bank—a feat that often prompted people to inquire about the secret to my success. Three key principles emerged from my experience:

1. Embrace Opportunities Beyond Your Role:
Never shy away from additional responsibilities. While not advocating for overloading oneself, exploring extra options opens doors to self-discovery and the acquisition of diverse skills.

2. Build and Leverage Your Network:
A strong network is an invaluable asset. Surround yourself with individuals who can help you achieve your goals and provide support when needed.

3. Emphasise the Power of Communication:
In a world inundated with emails, the spoken word holds immeasurable power. Relationships are nurtured and are developed more effectively through conversations rather than digital exchanges.

In addition to these principles, I realised the importance of crafting a personal brand. It wasn't just about what I said, it was about how I presented myself and the subtle actions that defined my character. I cultivated a reputation for being calm, reliable, honest, and notably, someone who rarely raised their voice.

Being perceived as calm and refraining from raising my voice, a trait often associated with femininity, wasn't always met with positive reception. Some deemed my demeanour as a hindrance, suggesting I needed to be louder, exude more gravitas, and restrain my positivity. These critiques, while demoralising, were instrumental in fostering moments of self-doubt and inviting imposter syndrome to take residence. The commentary implying that my approach was somehow insufficient or inappropriate due to its alignment with feminine qualities was disheartening. However, within this adversity, a seed of an idea germinated. It laid the foundation for my resolve to create a space, the Female Mentoring Alliance, where women could be appreciated for their authentic selves, regardless of societal expectations or biases.

The pivotal moment in my career came when I met with the Deputy CEO of the bank I was working in. Expressing my frustration and boredom with my current role, she suggested a complete shift. I applied for a position in a vastly different area, tasked with establishing a team to support her. This venture thrust me into the unknown, where I discovered my ability to set a vision and transform it into reality.

This move turned out to be the biggest risk I ever took—a leap into uncharted territory that ultimately defined my career. It taught me the importance of stepping out of my comfort zone, thinking beyond promotions and job strategies, and focusing on the broader picture of personal growth and fulfilment.

When I look back at my corporate career, I realise my journey exemplifies the power of embracing risks, building a strong brand, and seizing unexpected opportunities. It's a testament to the fact that sometimes, the most significant career achievements stem from the willingness to venture into the unknown and embrace the uncertainties that lie ahead.

Which is lucky as I then went on to take the biggest risk I ever have.

Breaking Barriers, Building Bridges: The Birth of the Female Mentoring Alliance

In the ever-evolving landscape of my career, the pivotal role of mentors has been a constant thread. These guiding figures, individuals who have navigated the paths I tread, provided insights, challenged my perspectives, and served as indispensable sounding boards. However, a turning point came when, as a newly appointed Managing Director, I found myself in a situation that sparked an unconventional vision for the future—an idea that would culminate in the formation of the Female Mentoring Alliance.

The catalyst for this initiative was a transformative course that urged us to shed traditional thinking and embrace a more entrepreneurial mindset. As part of this program, mentors were assigned to us, and I found myself paired with a Managing Director in risk—a seasoned professional, undoubtedly, but one whose approach and perspective couldn't have been more distant from what I needed. It was a moment of realisation—what if I had a mentor who had walked the unconventional path of a start-up, challenged norms and embraced innovation? And what if, on top of that, this mentor was a woman?

The concept began to take shape as I envisioned a community where women from diverse backgrounds could come together to mentor and support one another. The Female Mentoring Alliance was born out of a belief in the transformative power of women supporting women—a belief that had, at times, left me wanting within the traditional confines of my working world.

The allure of pairing a young banker with a mentor from the film industry to infuse creativity or connecting a designer with an engineer to stimulate new processes and logical thinking became a driving force. The idea wasn't to replicate career paths, but to create a tapestry of experiences and perspectives, fostering an environment where women could learn, share, and grow together.

I reflected on the instances when I had been surrounded by like-minded women. Strikingly, their backgrounds and careers varied widely, yet they were united by a shared commitment to support, nurture, and evolve. The Female Mentoring Alliance, in my mind, stood as a beacon for women from different walks of life, careers, and starting points to converge and embark on a collective journey of learning and empowerment.

The alliance aims to transcend the limitations imposed by traditional mentorship programs, encouraging unconventional pairings that could catalyse innovation and break down silos. It is a vision of a collaborative community where the exchange of ideas was not confined to a single industry but spanned the vast spectrum of human experience.

At the heart of the Female Mentoring Alliance lies a celebration of the profound power and strength inherent in being a woman. Here, femininity is not only embraced but exalted, recognising the unique gifts and qualities that women bring to the table. The alliance serves as a sanctuary where the nurturing instincts, empathy, resilience, and collaborative spirit intrinsic to womanhood are not only acknowledged but actively honed. Instead of conforming to societal norms or expectations, we empower women to authentically embrace their feminine attributes. By fostering an environment that champions the positive facets of being a woman, the Female Mentoring Alliance becomes a catalyst for personal and collective growth. Here, every woman is encouraged to embody her authentic self, and through this celebration, we craft a supportive community where the diverse strengths of women collectively shine.

I now needed to think about how I could make it happen and what I needed to do to bring this dream into a reality.

From Boardrooms to Blooms: A Journey of Transformation

Life often takes unexpected turns, and my journey from being a Managing Director in a bank to becoming a business owner, coach, and the architect of the Female Mentoring Alliance is a testament to the unpredictable nature of reinvention. This transformation didn't happen overnight; it began as a mere flicker of an idea, a persistent light on my shoulder that grew brighter over time.

The concept of the Female Mentoring Alliance started as a subtle notion—a nagging thought that evolved into a compelling vision. It took root during a conversation with a friend, another author in this book, sharing this collective narrative. Amidst the stress of potential redundancy, the idea surfaced, taking tangible form in our dialogue. Originally conceived as the Female Mentoring Association, it underwent a change prompted by peculiar legal constraints on the term "association." And so, the alliance was born, complete with a symbolic feather in its logo—a metaphorical flourish you'll unravel as we progress.

Simultaneously, driven by my innate commitment to rules and order, I embarked on dual paths. First, I delved into the realm of coaching, seeking qualifications and accreditation to augment my skill set and assure companies of my competence. Second, I dove into the intricate planning necessary to breathe life into the Female Mentoring Alliance. However, planning can be a double-edged sword; it often leads to inertia, a challenge I grappled with until unforeseen events reshaped my perspective.

The arrival of the COVID-19 pandemic brought about profound changes for my family. I transitioned into the role for the Deputy COO at the bank, abandoning the constant travel that had defined my career. This shift allowed me to be more present with my family, a reconnection that became a silver lining in the challenging times of lockdown. As the world gradually reopened, I returned to the office, but this period of readjustment also witnessed a seismic shift in my personal life.

The stability and routine I craved were disrupted by a harrowing experience—my husband, my rock, and love nearly died. Witnessing him vulnerable in a hospital bed compelled me to reassess everything. The political turmoil at work, the cuts, and the toxic atmosphere prompted me to make a bold decision. After 23 years in the corporate world, I chose to step away. Drawing a new structure where I wasn't a part of the equation, my husband and I decided to move to the countryside, embracing uncertainty and upheaval.

This marked the beginning of a fresh chapter. I transitioned from the familiar corridors of a corporate office to the uncharted terrain of entrepreneurship. Armed with the desire to push myself into the grey and open my imagination, I have started with one-on-one coaching and group coaching programs. TransformHER, a six-stage process I designed, aimed to empower women to take control of their desires and turn them into reality—a process mirroring my own journey.

Wings of Transformation: Soaring Beyond the Fear of Falling

As I pen down the final lines of this chapter, I'm filled with a sense of gratitude, reflection, and anticipation. The journey from a Managing Director in a bank to a business owner, coach, and founder of the Female Mentoring Alliance has been a tapestry of transformation, growth, and rediscovery.

Dear reader, at the start of this chapter, I shared my fear of falling—of taking that leap into the unknown. However, what I didn't reveal until now is my favourite phrase, the mantra that propels me forward: "What if I fall? Oh, but darling, what if you fly?" This empowering reminder adorns my necklace, is etched into the feather of the Female Mentoring Alliance logo, and echoes in my mind whenever doubt and old fears threaten to resurface.

I am deeply immersed in the world of coaching, a realm where I witness women undergo remarkable transformations, taking control of their lives through the six-stage process of TransformHER. Yet, even as I guide others, I am not immune to the uncertainties that the future holds. It is my once-again healthy husband who serves as my anchor, reminding me of the resilience we've cultivated together.

Our shared experiences, particularly the challenges that nearly cost us our togetherness, prompted a shift in priorities. We invested time in renovating our home and embraced a quieter life. Our dreams now extend to sharing our serene haven with others through an Airbnb in our field—a space for retreats, where a shepherd's hut overlooks rolling hills, offering a haven for peace and connection with nature.

In the midst of these changes, I've been reminded of the essence of my journey—the mentoring aspect that fuelled the inception of the Female Mentoring Alliance. Coaching and setting up our retreat took precedence, momentarily overshadowing the calling to bring women together.

However, the realisation has dawned, and I am ready to face it. The nerves surrounding logistics and setup have dissipated, making way for a renewed excitement to fulfil the original vision. The Female Mentoring Alliance is not just a platform; it's a community where women will come together in cohorts, exchanging the power of mentorship, support, learning, and dialogue. The vision statement resonates deeply: "The Female Mentoring Alliance brings women from all different backgrounds together. Through the power of mentoring, support, learning, and discussion, each woman will feel cherished and supported, allowing them to be truly unique."

This vision aligns seamlessly with the core belief of the Female Mentoring Alliance—that incredible things happen when women support women. As we approach the threshold of 2024, this year stands as a pivotal moment. While I continue with individual, group, and corporate coaching, I am set to launch the Mentoring Membership. It may start small, but with each member, it will blossom, receiving training, support, and nurturing to appreciate fully what it means to mentor and be mentored.

As I embark on this next phase, I invite you, dear reader, to follow along. The wings that symbolise transformation will continue to carry me forward, fuelled by the belief that every woman, when given the opportunity, can discover her unique brilliance and soar to unimaginable heights. This is not just a conclusion to a chapter; it's a prelude to a new beginning, where the Female Mentoring Alliance becomes a catalyst for countless stories of empowerment, growth, and connection.

LinkedIn: @thefemalementoringalliance
Website: www.thefemalementoringalliance.com

If you would like to find out how I can help you or be a founding member of the Female Mentoring Alliance, book a call.

https://calendly.com/thefemalementoringalliance/discovery-call

CHAPTER 14
Laura Davies
Managing Director & Founder - Marshall Harmony & MH Executive

Placing people first

I'm Laura, Founder & Managing Director of Marshall Harmony, an independent recruitment company placing talented individuals into successful businesses. Did I ever envision setting up my own business at the age of 40 with two wonderful children? Not at all. My aspirations had always been to be on stage; after all, I'm a trained singer with a background in method acting. So, how did I find myself as the owner and CEO of a successful & growing business? Let's journey back to the beginning.

The Genesis

There I was working for a major high street recruitment agency, unexpectedly sat in a boardroom with my manager. It was a meeting I wasn't looking forward to. I had been coerced into attending because "I had a nice tan." Even though it was my client, the meeting was regarding a situation in another part of our business, which I wasn't involved in. He was trying to save face based on my "relationship" with the client. I felt unprepared, undervalued and uncomfortable. It reinvoked feelings I hadn't felt since a traumatic incident at drama school.

I was led down steps into a cold, dark cellar that smelt damp and unnatural. "If you truly want to embody this character, you must walk in her shoes". I felt scared and uncomfortable, questioning whether it was all worth it.

It was in these moments I realised there must be a different way. In an almost epiphanous revelation, I realised that not only could I achieve my own goals but also help others achieve theirs without engendering compromising situations.

In my professional journey, integrity, transparency, and putting people first have been my guiding principles. However, in that suffocating boardroom atmosphere, something felt off—a misalignment of values. I couldn't believe what was being said, and I knew that I didn't want any part of it. The unspoken tension hinted at a clash that contradicted the core of what I hold dear professionally; my boss questioning me after the meeting on how I felt it had played out, his version of events being a far cry from mine. I felt frozen in time unable to escape. This wasn't where I wanted to be, but I couldn't just walk away, my family reliant on my income, I was trapped.

Unexpectedly, a turning point emerged, a call from the client acknowledging the value I bring as a recruiter. It served as a reminder that my professional worth isn't confined to the suffocating environment of that boardroom. Rewinding the tape on my 16-year recruitment journey, a path that found me bouncing from one temporary job to another, I experienced first-hand the positives and negatives of the recruitment industry when I walked back into a high street agency and was asked, "Have you ever considered recruitment"? I found myself in front of the person who would become my mentor and shape the ethos of the recruiter I became; the memories unfold like a series of scenes in my own film.

I had excelled throughout my career, winning awards, gaining recognition, and becoming the top performer in my company. I seemed to take to it like a duck to water, using my communication skills to actually engage and listen to people, treating them as human beings, rather than thinking of where my next bonus would come from. I recognised that accolades and recognition lose their meaning when they compromise the principles and values that define professional identity. A pivotal conversation with a headhunter who once sought me out became the catalyst for a life-altering decision. The idea of launching an independent agency under her company's umbrella emerged, and with a blend of uncertainty and excitement, I embarked on this uncharted journey, hoping to make a difference in an industry that doesn't always present itself or is perceived in the most positive of lights. Little did I know that this decision would set the stage (no pun intended) for a narrative that went beyond the desire for professional accolades.

The next three years unfolded with a maze of challenges, where would my clients come from? How do I manage finances? Can I pay myself? What if the business fails? But the most prominent in my life at that time were health concerns that tested the limits of my resilience. Amid the turbulence, I managed to sustain my business—through determination and a belief in the vision I was crafting. The challenges became threads woven into the fabric of my journey, shaping the narrative of resilience, adaptability, and tenacity.

Bouncing back from the shadows of illness, the pandemic struck, yet paradoxically for me, it became a new beginning. Infused with a renewed sense of energy and purpose, I continued to navigate the uncharted waters, fuelled by the lessons of the past and the resilience that defined my journey.

With the support of coaching, guidance, and family support, a new vision emerged—a business centred around family values. The inspiration was not abstract; it was personal. Our two children, the heartbeat of who we are, lent their names to the very core of our enterprise. During the chaos, their middle names became the foundation upon which we built a business rooted in purpose.

In the weeks leading up to this solo venture, a profound mindset shift occurred. It wasn't just about success or recognition; it was about aligning my values with my actions. A rekindled purpose, intricately connected to the tagline of my business, emerged: "placing people first." This wasn't merely a business venture; it was a manifestation of principles and a commitment to a meaningful existence.

As I navigated this desire, I realised that my commitment to integrity and placing people first wasn't just a tagline—it was the compass guiding my professional journey. The dimly lit boardroom, once a stage of discomfort, became the spotlight where I chose authenticity over conformity. It was a turning point, the opening scene of a narrative that transcended professional boundaries, an acknowledgement that professional success means little if it requires compromising the very values that define who I am in the real world.

It became a story of self-discovery, resilience, and the courage to forge a path guided by authenticity and a commitment to not leading candidates down those dark steps into the damp cellar.

The Motivation

Embarking on the journey of running my own business felt like standing at the cliff edge… the unknown.

Growing up in a family that cherished core values, I was surrounded by a unique blend of energy & commitment. Mum, a childminder, radiated vitality, and always prioritised my brother and I. Dad, a market trader, saw me as the apple of his eye. I'd join him at the crack of dawn, setting up my pasteboard to show my handmade jewellery. Dad, dedicated to his business, undoubtedly he put in long hours to provide for us. Reflecting on those years, I realise he missed out on some of our childhood adventures. Mum, on the other hand, was consistently there when I needed her. Dad's approach, though, stemmed from a deep belief in doing what he knew best to ensure the well-being of his family.

Dad was always great at getting to know his customers and suppliers, they would open up to him, he may have been selling them a wax jacket, but what he was really selling was a lifestyle.

And now the weight of responsibility, the success or failure of a business, rested solely on my shoulders, no safety net and mounting impending costs. The reality of entrepreneurship hit hard. With a foundation of a loyal client base, I found myself choreographing the intricate dance of filling job after job and attracting new clients eager to work with me.

In those early days, imposter syndrome crept in; despite building a career, who was I to tell a CEO of a multinational company who was and wasn't right for their business? Could I really do this? Casting shadows on my confidence.

Could I truly manage a business from my dining room table, adding value and developing effective relationships between clients with talented individuals? The doubt lingered, and as I took on more clients, word spread, and exhaustion set in. The hours spent working eclipsed the precious moments I craved with my family. It mirrored my childhood memories of a father who, as a market trader, was physically present but often emotionally absent, missing out on family trips and school events. I was determined not to replicate that pattern in my own family.

I was in a marriage with someone who prioritised family above all else, cherishing every moment together, and it became a cornerstone for me. We did everything as a unit, and it was profoundly meaningful. Ensuring our children experienced the presence of both parents at every step became a shared value, something I held dear in crafting a family grounded in togetherness.

The relentless pursuit of success had a familiar echo—my entrepreneurial spirit was deeply rooted. Drawing parallels to my childhood, I recognised that my innate ability as a natural salesperson, coupled with genuine empathy, set me apart. People seemed to open up to me effortlessly, sharing their challenges and aspirations. Having experienced personal difficulties growing up, and not always being accepted as a recruiter, this became my distinguishing trait—I cared genuinely, I believed ardently in forging crucial partnerships on a human level.

The paradox of success and sacrifice became glaringly apparent. Yes, I was building something noteworthy, expanding my client base, and making a mark within the industry. However, the toll on my personal life was undeniable. The metaphorical dining room table, once a symbol of entrepreneurial aspirations, became dichotomous, where work often overshadowed family time.

Amidst the chaos, a moment of clarity emerged. Entrepreneurship wasn't just a career choice; it was an inherent part of my identity. The exhaustion and self-doubt whilst challenging, were important hurdles on the path to creating a legacy and reinforcing the empathetic approach to the people that were rapidly making my business a success. I yearned to break the cycle of disconnection with those closest to me, steering away from the absenteeism I witnessed in my father.

It was a transformative realisation—one that propelled me to reassess my priorities. Yes, I was a natural salesperson, thriving on building relationships and connecting with people. However, the essence of success wasn't solely defined by financial gains; it rested in the delicate balance between professional pursuits and the invaluable moments with family.

As the business continued to grow, a renewed commitment to my family's well-being became the driving force. I understood that success, to be truly meaningful, needed to extend beyond the boardroom. The essence of being an entrepreneur was not just about making deals; it was about creating a harmonious life where genuine care and a commitment to all those who were helping to make me a success.

I felt fortunate that the ethos I was trying so hard to create was allowing my business to expand at a rate I never could have imagined at the start of the process, so with such rapid expansion, something had to change.

Learning to Let Go

Recognising the need for support in my business was one thing; figuring out what that looked like was a different challenge. I had so much experience in recruitment; bringing someone into my business would be a walk in the park, right? There were times in my professional career where I had questioned myself, leaving me feeling demoralised, it wasn't always a bed of roses. I found myself selecting individuals who didn't align with my vision, instead presenting formidable challenges.

Reflecting on both my personal and business life, my mother's advice echoed in my mind: "Keep something back, don't be too open, and let people in slowly." These words resonated deeply as I contemplated the next steps for my enterprise. Learning from past mistakes, I was determined not to replicate another version of myself. Instead, I sought someone who could complement my strengths and facilitate my aspirations, acting as a catalyst for the continuing expansion of the business.

Confronting the fear and imposter syndrome that haunted me, I initially postponed the idea of recruiting someone into the business. However, fate had other plans. During an interview for a client's customer sales role, I encountered Emily—an individual who would soon become an integral part of both my business and my life. Despite the preconceptions, I learned very quickly it's sometimes ok mixing business and leisure/pleasure.

Despite an uncomfortable conversation around my clients unwillingness to compromise on reduced hours to allow her the family time she craved, I had already identified her ability to connect, and what a valuable asset she would be to any business. This then led me to pose the question, that was presented to me at the beginning of my career "Have you ever considered a career in recruitment?" that unbeknown to me would alter the course of my business. An hour later, over coffee, we discovered shared values and a shared vision.

Walking to that meeting with Emily, uncertainty lingered, however. Was I truly ready for this collaboration? Did I want someone to step in and potentially take over aspects of the business I had kept so close to my chest? Conversations with other solo recruiters had left me both inspired and apprehensive. Yet, as I entered that meeting, a sense of empowerment enveloped me. I was proud of what I had built and ready to take charge, just like my clients did when interviewing potential employees.

Upon meeting Emily, it became abundantly clear—she was my missing piece. Aligned in family values and the desire for more meaningful time with loved ones, Emily not only embodied my business values but also exuded warmth and eagerness to learn. Her passion for her customers in the automotive industry mirrored my commitment to placing people first.

In that conversation about work, family, and life, it became evident that Emily was more than a potential team member—she was the person I had been searching for. Recognising the need for a compassionate intermediary to connect with job seekers, someone they could trust, I found my ideal collaborator in Emily, offering her the job on the spot. This moment marked not just the addition of a team member, but the beginning of a collaborative journey driven by shared values, mutual trust, and the genuine belief in the positive power of people.

Turning Threats into Opportunities

With Emily by my side, the prospect of taking on more clients and positioning myself at the forefront of networking events seemed within reach. However, the reality was that despite my theatrical training and confidence on stage, the mere idea of approaching strangers in a networking setting triggered an overwhelming sense of fear. Why did others believe in me more than I believed in myself? Why was I put on a pedestal?

Reflecting on a past accolade as the top performer in my first company, I remembered a pivotal moment in Athens where my husband questioned my tendency to hide. The fear of failure and the nagging question of "What if they don't like me?" haunted me. Standing tall in my own business became a necessity to break free from these self-imposed limitations.

As our business flourished, my focus shifted to more senior roles, yet I hesitated to let Emily directly interact with clients. She excelled at gaining candidates' trust, but I held onto the role of the intermediary. However, the universe had its plans, often revealed through unexpected twists, and my health became a catalyst for a pivotal business decision.

A sudden illness led to emergency surgery, forcing me to entrust my business entirely to Emily's capable hands. Even during my own health crisis, the dedication to my business remained. I found myself delegating tasks, even messaging a client from a hospital trolley en route to the operating theatre.

Post-surgery, I faced new challenges. Unbeknownst to me, I had been pushing people away, wearing a mask that concealed the internal struggles. Despite outward appearances, I grappled with personal difficulties.

Introduced to a coach by a friend, I embarked on a transformative journey. It became apparent that my idyllic childhood and the loss of my father at 25 had left lingering impacts. I unravelled the layers of rejection and events that had shaped my protective instincts, especially towards my daughter.

The fear of letting my guard down stemmed from past betrayals, making me wary of trusting others. Despite being considered a good judge of character, I acknowledged that this hadn't always been the case, I'd been hurt... I'd been let down. The journey toward dismantling the walls around me, lowering the mask, became a process of self-discovery.

The realisation that my business success was intricately linked to my personal growth became evident. Standing tall meant not just professional confidence but also addressing the layers of emotion and experiences that shaped my interactions. As I began to allow the mask to come down, I embraced the vulnerability that came with it, recognising that true strength lies not in the facade but in the authenticity of being wholly oneself.

Opening up more allowed me to integrate my ethos into the business, allowing me to exploit the essence of what was making it successful. The next chapter of my journey involved not just building a successful business but developing systems and practices that complimented what we had already achieved.

Looking in from the Outside

Emily and I excelled at "placing people first," yet when it came to administrative tasks and processes, it was more of a necessity than a source of enjoyment. The evolution of our workspace in my garden marked a significant milestone. Emily's creative design skills and my vision transformed it into a fabulous new home for Marshall Harmony, allowing a clear separation between business and home life—an aspect I had come to appreciate.

Our office, adorned with our brand colours and theme, became a special place, complete with a boardroom table and a breakout area for client interactions. It was the right time to bring in someone new to support the continuing expansion of Marshall Harmony. I could see, however, that Emily was somewhat hesitant to bring someone new into our world, our haven.

I interviewed a candidate, thinking they might fit, but Emily's discomfort made it clear that we needed to address whether it was the person or the idea of introducing someone new. It turned out to be the latter.

Empowering Emily with ownership over the responsibilities of anyone new that would join us, we sat down to brainstorm over lunch, crafting an extensive list of tasks. We agreed on seeking a part-time addition to our team, recognising the uniqueness of our partnership.

In a serendipitous moment, I stumbled upon Ellie's LinkedIn update about a new job. Having placed her as a PA three years earlier, I was intrigued by her next move. Connecting with Ellie on personal social media, a rarity for me, due to shared connections in my theatre world, I reached out. She hadn't started her new job, and during our conversation, I posed the same question I had asked Emily over a year earlier. Sending her the advert we had crafted, I invited her for coffee on the following Sunday, and the deal was sealed. I informed Emily of this spontaneous decision, and Ellie, due to start her new role the following week, quickly notified her intended employer of the change. Ellie's arrival in our office on Monday marked the beginning of a transformative dynamic. Ellie walked through the door, and the hug Emily gave her cemented their friendship immediately, showing me she had bought into the decision I'd made. The bond between Emily and Ellie, so different yet complementary, was instantly forged. They chatted over lunch as if they had known each other for years.

Ellie, the organising force we needed, swiftly identified efficiencies in our processes and cost savings. She seamlessly embraced our culture and values, fitting in like she had always been there. This was a pinch-me moment—with six children between us, I found myself responsible for improving the quality of life of these two incredible women, supporting their families.

As Marshall Harmony evolved into an organised trio, the harmony extended beyond our business operations, creating a sense of fulfilment and gratitude. The journey continued, marked by newfound dynamics and a shared commitment to growth, both personally and professionally.

Never Standing Still

Reflecting on my journey in the realm of recruitment unveils a tapestry of ups and downs. While the stories with clients and candidates could fill a book, the essence of my career has shaped the person I am today, and I hope the person I am today will shape the essence and success of my business in the future.

The trajectory, from a market trader's daughter with dreams of the West End stage to the woman standing here, has been marked by navigating through imposter syndrome, feeling like I'm not good enough. Today, I can enter a room authentically, with the mask down, embracing the unknown. There will be times where I must walk down those cellar steps again, I may even, on occasion, have to lead others there, only this time, hands will be held, and through empathy and communication, no one associated with my business will ever have to feel like I did that day in the boardroom or in the darkness on my own.

My achievements have transcended professional success; they have provided a foundation for my children, offering financial security beyond what I once deemed possible. Moreover, this journey has allowed me to continue to fulfil my dreams. I'm not just Laura the recruiter; I'm Laura the multifaceted woman—mother, wife, daughter, sister, friend, actress, and singer. I've grown more comfortable in my own skin, capable of standing up to those who once sought to knock me down, a strength I never found in my school days.

As Marshall Harmony embarks on an exciting new chapter, my focus has shifted to executive-level placements. Introducing the "Hire for Vision" model, I am working with existing and new clients to "place visionary leaders" that can drive success. This unforeseen development, now possible with the right team behind me, propels me not only to stand tall in recruitment but also in executive search. I am confident that my approach to partnerships and business relationships will thrive in this space, complementing the core of my recruitment business.

Looking ahead, I'm eager to share the insights and experiences encapsulated in my story. Each page is a testament to the journey of overcoming challenges, discovering strengths, and redefining success. This chapter, unveiling the layers of growth and transformation, closes with gratitude for the remarkable women who have been part of this narrative. On International Women's Day, may it inspire others on their journeys, celebrating the strength, resilience, and unity that define the spirit of women who dare to dream, persevere, and stand tall in their chosen paths.

Laura Davies: Managing Director & Founder - Marshall Harmony & MH Executive.

Website: www.marshallharmony.co.uk
LinkedIn: www.linkedin.com/in/lauradaviestoprecruiter

"Embrace the journey of unmasking, for it's only in wholeheartedly accepting ourselves that we remove the protective shield. Just as we must navigate the cold, dark cellar to truly appreciate the radiant light that awaits us." - Laura Davies

THE RISE OF THE FEMALE ENTREPRENEUR

CHAPTER 15
Jo Douglas
Menopause Support Mentor & Retreat Host

Where it all began: A Journey Rooted in Entrepreneurship

Growing up in an entrepreneurial household laid the groundwork for a path that became my own. From the tender age of 9, I started earning, cutting our family lawn and my neighbours. My dad, a man of diverse talents, initially had his own engineering business when I was a small child. However, he made a strategic decision to sell it, directing his focus to his passion for music and aspiring to become a professional musician. Meanwhile, my resourceful mum contributed by making all the stage costumes for my dad's band, effectively saving money. She also embraced the entrepreneurial spirit by running a

THE RISE OF THE FEMALE ENTREPRENEUR

Tupperware business, and an Avon business, hosting parties to showcase the innovative plastic food storage containers and beauty products—the first taste of Network Marketing in the family. In those early years. I braved the cold, going door to door, offering window cleaning services provided by my dad and canvassing, selling sacks of potatoes out of the back of my dad's van. It was a venture that not only topped up the family income but also marked the beginning of a dynamic partnership between us.

I left school at 17 with a modest collection of CSEs. Academics proved to be challenging for me with undiagnosed dyslexia. With a desire to explore the world, I got a job as a nanny in Egypt for a year (that was an eye-opening experience), saving all my money to return to England and embark on a backpacking adventure. I was uncertain of my future but fuelled by my love of travel.

During my travels, I found myself working in clubs and bars and distributing leaflets on the beach. A period I considered 'living the dream'. A pivotal moment occurred when a bar I worked in, trusted me to manage it while they flew back to the UK. My decision to host a nightly happy hour for the younger crowd resulted in double takings and a bustling bar, which the owners were very happy about on their return. In my naivety, I proudly declared myself a professional bar manager.

At the end of the summer, I returned home and shared my aspirations with my dad to buy a bar in Spain. Intrigue and perhaps living vicariously through my dreams, he remortgaged a property he had renovated, to lend me the money to go and buy myself a bar.

Skipping through a story that could fill pages, my life as the owner of 'The Cutty Sark Bar' in Mallorca. The UK was hit by a recession the same year. Leading to the closure of numerous hotels in the area. Faced with financial challenges and zero tourists, I built a local clientele of Spanish residents and British expats. Determined not to let my dad down, I closed the bar during the day after the first season, taking on additional jobs to make ends meet and working the bar in the evenings. Plus, I was sleeping on the pool table after giving up my apartment. I entered my 20s with a resilient spirit driven by the commitment to repay my dad and honour my financial obligations.

Rent a Crowd, it Was Me or Them

In the midst of the recession and the closure of many bars and restaurants in the area, desperate times called for creative solutions. By day, I was working for a timeshare company, shuttling curious tourists from Magaluf beach to a small resort town 20 minutes away. The return trip was often met with frustration from disappointed tourists, who felt they had wasted their day for mere free tickets to a water park. By night, I turned on the smile, doing my best to keep my customers returning, putting on different events every night of the week, and trying very hard to entice the expat community into my bar.

My wages from this job, combined with income from cleaning a few apartments barely covered the rent for the bar. I was sleeping only a few hours a night between the pool table and my Spanish boyfriend's place, and putting a smile on for my punters was becoming increasingly hard. I put The Cutty Sark up for sale, but the likelihood of it selling was slim in an area where lots of other bars and hotels had already closed. I needed a plan to get rid, I couldn't lose it, I couldn't let my dad down.

Turning to the expats I worked with at the timeshare and the yachtie crowd (the term we used for customers who worked on super yachts in the Port of Palma), I made a bold proposition. I asked them if they would all frequent my bar on the nights' potential buyers were visiting, offering them half-price drinks all night. The result was transformative. A bustling bar filled with expats, music playing and people laughing, a buzzing atmosphere that mirrored my initial vision for The Cutty Sark.

A couple from Liverpool seized the opportunity and bought the bar. As the transfer took place, a wave of emotion swept over me-tears of relief, knowing I could finally repay my dad and step away from the gruelling day and night work schedule. Yet that lingered a profound sense of guilt for the buyers. The deception weighed heavily on my conscience, and even now, decades later, the memory stirs a sense of regret. In an era before meticulous bookkeeping, they barely made it through one season before closing down and cutting their losses. The experience, though tinged with remorse, was a profound chapter in my five-year journey of being a bar owner.

Feeling the weight of my actions and needing a fresh start, I made the decision to leave Mallorca before the lovely scouse couple discovered the truth. To them, if they ever come across these words, I offer my sincere and eternal apologies.

Travel, everything I always wanted to do

In search of a new chapter, I heard about a job on a yacht, and without hesitation, off I went on a journey that could fill another book. My days as a "yachtie" began with extensive travel, and I dedicated myself to taking numerous courses over the years to climb the ranks on board. The charter guests aboard the yacht asked us to find a massage therapist to join us for the remainder of the trip, but none were available. This got me thinking. I had a chat with the captain, sharing that I had experienced a few massages in my time and believed I could handle the task. That evening, as we docked in Ft Lauderdale, I sought out a massage therapist. In an era very different from 2024, back in the late '90s, I paid for a 2-hour crash course while the guests were away for dinner. Confident in my abilities, I purchased a massage table and set it up in one of the cabins. For the remainder of the trip, my role transformed into the on-board massage therapist, a role I embraced wholeheartedly. The positive feedback from satisfied guests and generous tips prompted me to consider a career change. I enrolled in a nine-month, full-time massage and nutrition course in Ft Lauderdale.

My newfound skills opened doors to a position on a larger yacht, where I served as the designated massage therapist for the owner and their esteemed guests. This fulfilling role continued until I received the joyous news of my pregnancy aged 35. Opting to leave the yachting world behind, I embraced marriage and transitioned into the rewarding role of a full-time mum. Together with my husband, we embarked on a shore-based life, navigating the globe with our two young boys in tow. However, my husband remained in the yachting industry, steadily advancing his career to eventually become a Captain. This commitment kept him away for extended periods, and he would only join us when the boat was in port or when he took holidays. (He is still away for six months of the year, on a rotation of 2 on and 2 off). Over the years, we embraced the richness of life in five different countries until finally settling in the UK to provide a stable environment for our boys to complete their schooling.

Today, those boys have grown into individuals enriched by diverse cultures, aged 14 and 19.

One of those countries we lived in was Qatar. We enrolled the boys into an international school, and I did more courses to enable myself to work in their school. I became a support teacher for children with additional needs. There was one boy in particular who I will never forget. He needed me to get into the pool with him when they had their swimming lessons, I really enjoyed these sessions, and I knew the school were looking for another swimming coach, so I offered to get qualified to take on this role. Offer accepted. I then climbed the ladder to head coach at King's College Doha. I was also studying to be a Level 3 Early Years teacher; I enjoyed this age group the most.

Qatar is where I discovered Aloe Vera products. One of the mums from my boys' rugby club was a distributor with Forever Living. Intrigued, I learned about the incredible benefits of drinking Aloe Vera. She also introduced me to some excellent weight loss products, which became my go-to after every holiday. It provided a fantastic cleanse for my overindulgent holiday body. Drinking Aloe Vera daily became a cornerstone of my wellness routine, and I found myself feeling remarkably healthy and fit – probably the healthiest I had ever been in my entire life. I also fell in love with Pilates. The transformation in my health from our days living in Europe and the early days in Qatar was truly incredible.

Perimenopause hit, but I didn't know it

Reflecting on the past, it's clear to me now – though it wasn't then - that I was navigating perimenopause without the crucial support I needed. It's almost surreal to think I nearly walked away from my wonderful and supportive husband during that challenging period. At the height of perimenopause, around the age of 47/48, I found myself engulfed in mood swings and frustrations. Lee, bless him, became the unwitting target of my irritations. It seemed everything he did rubbed me up the wrong way, and he couldn't catch a break. I was short-tempered, and in my mind, it was all his fault. I couldn't fathom why he seemed so irritating. We were growing apart, and our relationship was strained. It took Lee's suggestion of seeking marriage guidance to bring us back from the brink.

We were met with disbelief – after all, we didn't have a clear reason for our troubles. However, the therapist guided us to listen to each other and rediscover the reasons we fell in love. Little did I know that my fluctuating oestrogen levels were at the root of my disdain for my ever-loving husband. Thankfully, we weathered that storm, it was a challenging time, the night sweats were ridiculous too, changing my sheets every day and sometimes in the middle of the night led to tiredness, which didn't help my mood. I was undeniably a different person.

Cleaning up my diet, incorporating regular exercise, and - recommended by the therapist – embracing mindfulness were the keys to steering us back on course. Looking back, I can honestly say I love him more now than I ever have. This journey has taught me the importance of recognising the signs and seeking support, it is SO important.

It's evident that I experienced a myriad of symptoms, even before my second child was born. When son #1 was around three years old, I began grappling with night sweats, this was getting in the way of trying for a second child. I was only 38, too young for menopause SURELY, but at this point, menopause wasn't even in my mind, and I had never heard of perimenopause.

Eventually, I did fall pregnant with son #2. We moved to France, and while adjusting to life with two small boys and a husband away an awful lot, I was blindsided by a severe bout of vertigo. It was overwhelming, doctors were baffled as to what was causing it. It came and went for about a year. Looking back now, knowing vertigo is a perimenopause symptom, I can see a pattern of bouts occurring when my diet was not at its best, and I wasn't exercising. I wish I knew then, what I have learned these last few years. This is why I am passionate about getting the word out and helping as many women as I can. If my experience resonates with you, perhaps it's time to consider the possibility of perimenopause. Recognising the problem is the first step towards finding a solution.

Lockdown: My Dive into a New Business Adventure

It was 2020 in Devon, a beautiful part of the UK! I'm immersed in the world of managing a breakfast and after-school club at the local primary school when the unexpected lockdown unfolds. Fortunately, my husband Lee is locked down with us. Spare a thought for the poor captain he rotates with – stuck on the boat during these challenging times.

In one of the warmest Springs England had witnessed in years, we found ourselves in a fortunate position, with a lovely garden to revel in. We had BBQs, drinks, and more drinks, and the simple joy of being together as a family became our daily rhythm. While the world faced a sad and daunting situation, we remained cocooned in our bubble, only turning on the news for updates. I can't help but feel a pang of guilt acknowledging our enjoyment amidst the global struggles, fully aware of the profound loss and suffering many faced.

Enough was indeed enough. As the lockdown lingered into the summer, my waistband was expanding, and the pesky perimenopausal symptoms were staging a comeback. Just because the BBQ was getting a workout, the sun was shining, and work was on pause didn't mean we had to indulge our way through summer. Time for a reset!!

I reached out to my Aloe Vera Lady, Marie in Qatar, asking if she knew how I could get my hands on a 9-day cleanse program and some Aloe Vera here in the UK. To my surprise, she shared that she had an online shop, and the products are available worldwide. Amazed by this revelation, I delved into the cleanse and gradually regained my health. Symptoms were easing, and both my appearance and well-being improved.

While on the 9-day cleanse, I documented my fitness journey on Facebook. With the lockdown keeping many more people glued to social media, my posts gained traction. Friends flooded my inbox, eager to know where they could purchase this program. In a lightbulb moment, I called Marie asking how to become a distributor, and thus, the seed of entrepreneurship sprouted. Facebook could be the platform to spread the word and make these health-boosting products accessible to friends and beyond. My Network Marketing journey began.

You have probably worked it out by now; even though I left school scraping through with only a few exams, I am a lifelong learner, continually seeking knowledge to propel my career forward.

I found myself having lots of conversations with friends about menopause, particularly perimenopause. A realisation dawned on me as to why I felt off during my time in France and in the initial years in Qatar. Ahh, perimenopause, that explains it. Delving into research, I discovered the intricate link between perimenopausal symptoms and overall wellness. Recognising the positive impact of a healthy lifestyle on my well-being, I embarked on more courses.

Drawing on my background in nutrition from my yachting days, I pursued a Level 4 qualification in nutrition as well as accredited wellness and menopause courses. As I began providing advice to friends, recommending Aloe Vera for gut health, and the Mediterranean diet to support their hormones, the foundation of my coaching business took shape. Today, I can proudly say, I am a Menopause Support Mentor, feeling immense joy from helping women rediscover themselves. Witnessing their empowerment through lifestyle changes I helped and supported them with, fills me with a profound sense of purpose and satisfaction.

From Cleanses to Coaching: Unveiling the Midlife Harmony Retreats

Let's backtrack a second, where did my Midlife Harmony Retreat come from? During my pregnancy with my firstborn, Lee was away, and I found myself house-hunting in Spain. Andalusia captured my heart, and much of my pregnancy was spent at my best friend Jilly's house, nestled in the Sierra de las Nieves mountains. Jilly, also expecting, shared her home with me, her poor hubby had two pregnant women to look after. While exploring houses in the region with the help of my dad, I realised that being up in the mountains, though breath-taking, was a bit too secluded for my liking. The foothills felt like the perfect balance between natural beauty and proximity to civilisation. We spent many a day driving around bumpy tracks looking at property after property. Many of them had their charm, but none felt quite right. Then, the estate agent showed us a hidden gem, it needed a lot of work, but it had a distinct energy about it. We just looked at each other and smiled. Dad felt it too. The energy was strong, and yes, it was perfect. We put an offer in after a phone call to hubby to tell him we had found the perfect place.

Fast forward eight months, Lee and I were getting married in Mallorca when son #1 was six months old. We received a phone call on our wedding day, our haven was finally ours. The perfect wedding present, it was meant to be. With its rustic charm and a sanctuary of renewal, balance, and energy. Unbeknown to me, it was the seeds of the Midlife Harmony Retreat.

Over the years we spent time, energy, and money on our piece of paradise. When we weren't living there or holidaying there, we let others enjoy what it offered, letting it out for holiday lets (We still do). We named it Douglas Creek. The land has a small creek running through it, separating it into two parts. My dad lived in a yurt on one side, and Douglas Creek is on the other. My dad looked after everything while we were still moving around with Lee's job. I take the online bookings and he would greet them on arrival. Dad was there for five years when he decided to move back to the UK. Our friends Belen and Ale moved into the yurt to take over, and the yurt grew into a small three bed annexe for their growing family of 4.

It really is a special place. Belen and her family have a special place in my heart, looking after our home like it's their own.

One Summer a couple of years ago, we were having a BBQ, with my family and Belen's. I said I would love to bring my clients here and mentor them over a weekend or a week, and include some yoga and meditation. We could have massages and facials and learn about the right nutrition. Belen said yes, 'we could all cook together'- we talked on into the night about all the wonderful therapists and wellness experts who lived in the area, they could co-host, and we could run wonderful empowering intimate retreats here. And so 'Midlife Harmony was Born'.

THE RISE OF THE FEMALE ENTREPRENEUR

I am hosting four retreats a year; I am still living in Devon, but the plan is to move back to Spain when my youngest has finished school. My vision is to host at least double that amount, as well as continue mentoring and supporting women online. I am still evolving as an entrepreneur, I am also now a Tropic ambassador, because I love the toxin free skin care and use it on my guests at the retreats, the ladies absolutely love it. My facials are part of your self-care, as well as a full-body massage. I have wonderful co-hosts helping me, and ladies are leaving my retreats feeling rejuvenated and empowered with a plan of action.

If you want to experience the energy of a Midlife Harmony Retreat or need support and mentoring to make those important changes in your lifestyle, to feel the best you can be, let's embrace midlife together, get in touch, and we can get your journey started!

"Thank you so much for sharing your beautiful retreat with us. Such a wonderful place to get re-connected to myself. You have a lovely personality, I felt instantly comfortable, and left nourished and inspired in many ways. Ready to continue the good work of looking after myself and enjoy this stage of my life. Thank you so much. I would definitely recommend your retreat to my friends. Lots of love and many blessings, Nat xx".

Jo Douglas
Menopause Support Mentor and Retreat host as seen on FOX TV
LinkTree: https://linktr.ee/jodouglas

CHAPTER 16
Jo Mould
YES! Life Girl & 7 Figure Badass

Why I Decided to Start YES! Life

What if I told you that you could craft the exact life you desire, a life that feels like pure magic, an undeniable YES! Life? The truth is, you can, and you should. The world is waiting for you to step into that life, that version of yourself. Because if we all wait for someone else to do it, or for someone else to do it for us, we risk living a half life.

Let me share my YES! Life story, a journey from the belief that success meant relentless hard work to a life where every box, including love, relationships, health, fun, and travel, is a perfect 10. Growing up, my father, a highly successful entrepreneur, ingrained in me the idea that immense success required ceaseless dedication. I watched him work tirelessly, leaving little room for anything else. This became my 'normal,' the 'only way.' Following in his footsteps, I adopted the same workaholic lifestyle, thinking it was the key to financial prosperity.

However, I soon realized that having only my 'work' box checked at 10/10 wasn't fulfilling. I craved more - a life where all my boxes were 10/10. Why not? Us women can have it ALL. Isn't that why we ventured into business? To have the freedom to choose, the money to say YES, and the ability to decide where we live.

Now, in my version of the YES! Life, I reside by the beach, working when I want, on what I want. Daily, I surround myself with those I choose, and the best part... I get to say YES to every opportunity that presents itself.

However, this YES! Life wasn't a sudden revelation. It required me to navigate the path from where I was to where I wanted to be. I had to acquire the skills to create my YES! Life and, most importantly, embrace the notion that it gets to be easy. This concept was a mental challenge, especially after conditioning myself for 30-odd years to believe in the 'you have to work hard' story.

But here I am, living proof that you can get there too. I'm excited to show you how, so you can arrive at 'EASY' because, honestly, life is just way more fun here!

Your version of the YES! Life might look different, and that's absolutely okay. I extend my love to whatever it is you want your YES! Life to look like. It could be a bustling city, a serene countryside, or anything in between.

As you embark on this journey, remember that creating your YES! Life doesn't happen overnight. It's a process that involves learning the necessary skills and rewiring your mindset. The most challenging part might be accepting that it gets to be easy, but trust me, it's worth it.

So, let's dive into the secrets, the mindset shifts, and the skills that propelled me from a life of hard work to one of ease and enjoyment. Together, let's make your YES! Life a reality, because life is undeniably more enjoyable when you embrace the magic and say YES to everything you desire. And believe me, you get to be much more BADASS in this place.

How I Started My Business

In the journey of life, there are moments when we stand at the crossroads, faced with decisions that could shape our destiny. What if, instead of shying away from the unknown, we embraced the challenge? What if we said YES! to the opportunities that scare us, worked out the 'how' later, and refused to let the fear of the unknown dictate our path?

Coco Chanel once said, "A woman should be two things - what and who she wants." This quote embodies the essence of living a YES! Life. It's about breaking free from societal expectations, embracing authenticity, and fearlessly pursuing our desires.

The heart of the matter lies in doing the things that scare us. It's in those moments of discomfort, stepping outside our comfort zones, that true growth and transformation occur. Saying YES! to challenges, even when we don't have all the answers, is a declaration of self-confidence and a commitment to personal evolution. Saying YES! without knowing the 'how' is what us badass women learn to embrace!

A crucial aspect of living a YES! Life is understanding that not saying NO to something unwanted is akin to saying YES. It's about setting boundaries and choosing a life aligned with our deepest desires. This principle empowers us to shape our reality consciously and intentionally, cultivating a life that resonates with our true selves.

What excites me most about this philosophy is the profound impact it has on our happiness and magnetism. Living a YES! Life makes us resilient. The trivialities that may bother others become insignificant, and we navigate challenges with grace. Road rage diminishes, and hatred fades away. We become kinder, more compassionate individuals. We become, in my opinion, better people to be around.

Imagine a world where everyone lives their YES! Life.

It's a world of authenticity, joy, kindness and FUN. This vision fuels my passion, and I believe it could create a more beautiful world for us, our children, and our grandchildren. A legacy worth leaving.

Contrary to societal norms, we are not bound to accept a life dictated by others. We don't have to endure jobs we hate or reside in places that stifle our spirits. What if your daily grind wasn't a grind at all? How much happier and fulfilling could your life be? How would your relationships with your spouse and children flourish if you woke up excited about your day?

The decision to write this chapter about a YES! Life came unexpectedly, in the confined space of an aeroplane toilet cubicle. It was a moment of revelation, a message from the universe that I couldn't ignore. Despite initial doubts about the importance of my message and the perceived effort of writing this chapter, I knew the world needed to hear it.

Reflecting on that moment still gives me goosebumps and brings tears to my eyes. It was a turning point, a call to elevate and step into my greatness. Each tear, each emotion, underscores the authenticity and urgency of the message I carry. It's a call for women to rise above the daily grind, listen to their intuition, and embrace their true selves.

When we're trapped in a life that doesn't align with our YES! Life, we often miss the messages and intuitions guiding us towards something greater. The daily grind keeps us stuck in our heads, weaving scenarios that may not even be real. My sincere desire is for women to break free from this mental entrapment, to step into the beautiful beings they are, and to become the women the world desperately needs.

I encourage women to join me on this journey of fearlessness and empowerment. Say YES! to your desires, work out the 'how' later, and watch as your YES! Life unfolds before you. It's time to step out of your head, embrace your greatness, and become the woman you were meant to be. You are a Badass after all.

Claim your YES! Life

Embracing Ease, Manifestation, and Magnetism

Do you wake up excited for your day, eager to embrace the possibilities that lie ahead? Or do you find yourself trapped in a cycle of hustle, wondering if there's a way to make life more enjoyable and less overwhelming? What if I told you that it gets to be easy – that you have the power to leverage your life for maximum fulfilment and success?

Let's start with a fundamental question: What are you doing in your life that someone else could be doing? It's time to embrace the power of outsourcing. As a true badass, it's essential to focus on what you do best and delegate the rest. Free up your time and energy for the things that truly matter, both in your personal life and your business.

Does your business demand your attention 24/7? It's time to reassess and implement systems that allow your business to thrive without your constant presence. Leverage technology, delegate tasks, and create a business model that works for you, not the other way around.

Now, let's dive into the realm of manifesting and becoming Magnetic AF. Manifesting is the key to creating your YES! Life. It's about consciously attracting the life you desire through the power of intention and belief. But it doesn't stop there. Becoming Magnetic AF is the natural outcome when you claim your YES! Life.

Setting BIG, juicy goals is the first step to manifesting your dreams. These goals should be so audacious that they scare you – if they don't, they're not big enough. Remember, you are not here to play small. Playing small doesn't serve you, your family, your business, your impact, or the world.

Now, let's talk about scripting your YES! Life. Once you've set your big, juicy goal, create a detailed script envisioning your future. What day is it? What has happened? How are you feeling? Where are you? Who are you with? Immerse yourself in the script, infusing it with the emotions you'd experience in that future reality. Make it a habit to listen to your script daily – attach it to a routine, like your daily shower.

Energy is everything in this journey. It's not about fake high energy but cultivating authentic, high-vibe energy. When your energy is elevated, your magnetic resonance is enhanced, drawing similar energies and opportunities toward you. Becoming magnetic is like unlocking a magical dimension of your life.

Consider the analogy of magnets – they attract what is similar to them. When you truly step into the work, owning your desires, and doing the necessary work, you become magnetic. It's a transformation that feels almost magical.

I used to think manifestation was reserved for the select few who possessed some innate ability. However, my journey taught me otherwise. If I can do it, so can you. All it takes is a burning desire to become magnetic, seeking the right knowledge, surrounding yourself with the right people, and committing to the work.

As you embark on this journey to leverage your life, remember: it gets to be easy, you get to manifest your dreams, and becoming magnetic is within your grasp. Step into the magic, claim your YES! Life, and watch as the universe aligns with your desires.

Badass Circle: Elevate Or Settle? The Deeper Truth Unveiled

In the age of online connections and virtual relationships, the saying "you are the sum of the five people you spend the most time with" takes on a profound meaning. It's not merely about physical presence; it extends to the voices and messages you allow into your life, shaping your thoughts, beliefs, and ultimately, your destiny. As we navigate this digital era, who you follow on social media, the videos you consume, the podcasts you listen to, all contribute to your circle, both physical and non-physical.

Guarding your mental and emotional space becomes imperative. Women who've manifested their dream lives understand the significance of curating their influences. They are discerning about the voices they allow into their world, whether it's a physical gathering or an online community. What groups are you part of? Are they filled with individuals doing the work, striving for more, or do they resonate with unhappiness and resistance to change?

The impact of your circle on your life is profound. Your potential for impact is enormous, but playing a bigger game is essential. The world needs you to step into your greatness. You have one life. What would you be doing today if you could do anything? Life is precious, and the one thing you want so badly it makes you feel sick - have you done it? What could your life look like on the other side of that courageous decision? Almost always, everything you desire is on the other side of fear.

It's disheartening to witness women avoiding the very thing they yearn for, settling for a half-lived life. Life becomes extraordinary when you muster the courage to pursue that which you desire. Remember, the enemy of an extraordinary life is a good life. By playing small, you inadvertently impact those around you. Conversely, when you claim the big life you deserve, you give others permission to do the same. A magical domino effect.

Now, let's talk about Magnetic Ease—the ability to attract and manifest your desires effortlessly. Playing big is not just a personal necessity; it's a service to the world. Keeping your magnetism high is key to manifesting your YES! Life. For some, it's dancing or walking on the beach; for others, it's setting big, juicy goals that excite them, scripting those goals into reality, and being around people who not only encourage a big life but hold them accountable.

Here's a surprising revelation: you can teach yourself how to manifest while experiencing a big, juicy O! It's a testament to the magical connection between pleasure, desire, and manifestation. Go on, try it. I dare you!

In conclusion, your circle is not just about who you physically spend time with but extends to every voice, message, and influence in your life. Embrace the power of a badass circle that challenges you to elevate, to play a bigger game, and to claim the extraordinary life you deserve. Let your impact be profound, your magnetism high, and your life an inspiring journey toward your YES! Life.

Subconscious Reprogramming: Change Your Thinking, Change Your Life

In a world filled with stress, dissatisfaction, and the incessant pace of life, the call to play big, to live with self-confidence and joy, reverberates louder than ever. The question arises: how do we achieve rapid and transformative change? The answer lies in the realm of Subconscious Reprogramming, a powerful force that has profoundly altered my life, offering the promise of a brighter, more fulfilled existence.

RTT® is a revolutionary approach to therapy that delves into the subconscious mind, uncovering and reprogramming deep-seated beliefs that shape our reality. It's a process that makes us suggestible, opening the door to profound transformation by addressing the root causes of our challenges. I've found it to be the easiest work we can do on ourselves, as it empowers us to change our thinking effortlessly.

As I reflect on the impact of RTT® on my life, tears well up in my eyes. It's not just about personal success; it's about creating a world where individuals are happy with themselves and radiate joy. The prevalence of people absorbed in their devices, escaping from reality, paints a dismal picture of our present world. The yearning for a future where individuals confidently engage with the world, smiling at strangers and loving their lives, drives me to share the profound impact of Subconscious Reprogramming.

Quite honestly, RTT® has enabled me to experience quantum leaps in my business and life goals.

I envision a world where individuals break free from mundane jobs that drain their joy, where relationships thrive, and where happiness is not a distant dream but a daily reality. Marriages strained by financial stress and the relentless grind would find solace, and families would revel in moments of genuine connection. This vision isn't just a personal desire; it's a call for a collective transformation, a world where joy and fulfilment become the norm.

In the face of these challenges, I believe it starts with us. While we cannot control the world, we have absolute control over ourselves. The legacy I aspire to leave behind is one where people harness the power to change their thinking and, in turn, change their lives. Our control over ourselves is the key to transforming the world we live in. It's a journey toward joy, happiness, and a life well-lived, one that radiates positivity, touches hearts, and sets the stage for a brighter future for generations to come.

As we embark on this transformative journey, let's envision a world where each smile, each expression of love, and each moment of genuine connection contributes to a ripple effect of joy. It's not just about us living our YES! Life; it's about co-creating a world where joy becomes the language of humanity.

You Are a Badass!

Life is an intricate tapestry woven with threads of relationships, experiences and connections. It's these human bonds that truly define our existence, providing meaning, joy, and purpose. I want to share a personal story that reshaped my perspective on life, underscoring the profound impact of human connection. This is a story about my brother, a journey through grief, and the transformative power of embracing a 'Yes' life.

When we reflect on what truly makes us happy, it's not the material wealth, the fame, or the accolades. It's the power of human connection that stands at the forefront. In our daily lives, we often overlook the simple yet profound moments of connection – a smile shared with a stranger, a conversation in an elevator, or a random encounter on public transport. These instances might seem inconsequential, but they possess the magic to elevate our spirits and bring joy to the mundane.

Life can take unexpected turns, and for me, the catalyst for a monumental shift was the sudden loss of my brother. His departure forced me to confront the fragility of life and question the choices I was making. It prompted a deep reflection on the meaning of happiness and fulfilment. In the face of grief, I realised the importance of embracing a life that resonated with my true desires.

As I navigated the grieving process, I recognized the urgent need to break free from the confines of a 'No' life. A life where opportunities were dismissed, connections were avoided, and the pursuit of genuine joy was hindered by fear and complacency. My brother's passing from leukaemia when he was just 34 years old became a stark reminder that life is finite, and I owed it to myself and his memory to live authentically. I owed it to Mikey to live a BIG AF life.

During moments of profound loss, human connection emerged as a healing balm. Friends, family, and even strangers played a pivotal role in helping me navigate the complex emotions of grief. Their empathy, shared stories, and genuine connections became the foundation upon which I started rebuilding my life. It was through these connections that I rediscovered the beauty of vulnerability and the strength derived from shared human experiences.

One of the most transformative aspects of embracing a YES! Life was summoning the courage to engage with the unknown. Striking up conversations with strangers, whether in an elevator or on public transport, became a source of joy rather than fear. The unfamiliar became an opportunity for connection, understanding, and shared humanity. I realised that within the unknown lies the potential for some of the most beautiful and enriching experiences life has to offer.

As I stepped into this new chapter of embracing life with a resounding 'YES,' I noticed a profound ripple effect. The joy and courage I experienced through human connection became contagious. By allowing myself to be vulnerable, authentic, and open to the richness of shared experiences, I inadvertently inspired others to do the same. It reinforced the idea that our choices not only shape our individual narratives but have the power to influence the collective narrative of those around us.

So, I encourage you to embrace the power of human connection in your own life. Say 'YES' to conversations, to shared moments, and to the beautiful unknown. In doing so, you might just discover a wellspring of joy and fulfilment that transforms not only your life but the lives of those you touch along the way. After all, it's the tapestry of human connections that makes our journey truly extraordinary.

It was fourteen months ago, in the confined space of an aeroplane toilet cubicle, a tiny idea took root in my mind. Little did I know that this seemingly insignificant moment would blossom into a reality that I am now experiencing today, thousands of feet above the ground. As I sit on another plane, immersed in the pages of the final draft for this YES! Life chapter, tears stream down my face – tears of happiness, tears of joy, tears of disbelief. This is not just my chapter; it's a testament to the power of turning dreams into reality.

It all started with a quiet moment in an aeroplane restroom, in those fleeting minutes, I realised that I had a story to tell, a book within me waiting to be written. It was a whisper of inspiration that sparked a fire within, urging me to put pen to paper and give life to my thoughts and experiences.

As with any creative endeavour, doubt became a companion on my journey. Within four months of conceptualising the book, my internal critic - the imposter - emerged.

Questions showed up: Did my story have value? Would it resonate with others? Was I good enough to share my narrative with the world? These doubts threatened to overshadow the initial spark of inspiration.

Addressing the imposter within is a crucial step in any creative process. I acknowledged the doubts but refused to let them dictate the course of my journey. I recognized that these internal voices were not my friends but frenemies, attempting to hold me back from reaching my full potential. It was time to silence the doubt and embrace the BADASS within.

To anyone facing their own doubts and hesitations, I offer a simple message: do the things. Those dreams that seem insurmountable, the goals that appear out of reach — pursue them with unwavering determination. Live a life that refuses to be confined by limitations. Don't settle for mediocrity, and, most importantly, don't let the voices in your head dictate your destiny.

Each of us possesses a reservoir of strength and resilience. It's time to tap into that badassery and live a life that aligns with our deepest desires. Your YES! Life is not a distant dream; it's an urgent matter. Embrace the challenges, do the hard things, celebrate the victories, and don't let the fear of inadequacy slow you down.

You are a Badass. You are magnetic AF. Go claim your YES! Life.

Connect with me – https://jomould.groovepages.com/connectwithjo

YES! Life Money Facebook Group - https://www.facebook.com/groups/3760538947340324

Book a YES! Life Call with Me - https://calendly.com/jomould/yes-life-call?month=2024-01

Website: https://jomould.com

Sales Badassery™ - https://www.nwmwomen.com/salesbadassery

YES! Life Retreat - https://members.nwmgenius.com/wp-content/uploads/2023/09/YES-Life-Retreat.pdf

Onlinepreneur Club - https://onlinepreneurclub.com.au/

THE RISE OF THE FEMALE ENTREPRENEUR

CHAPTER 17
Ali Braid
Owner/ L & D Consultant for the Recruitment Industry

I grew up in a Buckinghamshire town, and my parents both worked full-time. Dad was a franchise owner of a business estate agency. My mum was an English teacher and, over time, Head of Department in various state and private schools nearby. I had a lovely childhood, and my brother and I were always looked after and had what we needed. The 1980-82 recession did have an effect on our household, and I know now that both my parents had periods of intense worry about money. But we never would have known, and the house was always full of laughter, of friends and grandparents visiting and babysitting.

My Nan was a huge supporter of everything I did. When my grandad passed away, my parents built a granny annex for her. She was always a brilliant sounding board, and even though she passed away 15 years ago, I often imagine what her advice would be and do that. She was hugely intelligent, and her emotional intelligence was outstanding. We often wonder what she would have done if she'd been born later. A part of the land army, she lost her first love as he was in the RAF and never made it home. So my grandad proposed, and the rest is history.

My Nan and grandad always had a business- they ran a hotel in Aviemore, Scotland, an antique shop, a post office in the Cotswolds and in their retirement, they had an antique business again. My Nan would often keep her favourite bits of furniture, so their flat was filled with stuff that she would say would never sell. Both my grandparents were entrepreneurs, and I hope they would be proud of me.

I wanted to be a teacher from a very early age, and I would make my little brother come to "school" while I wrote things on a mini chalkboard.

After my A levels (history, art, English), I went to Warwick University, where I studied a combined degree of English literature with a teaching qualification. We were very quickly in schools teaching children (too soon, some may say looking back), and I loved it. We were doing the job whilst our fellow roommates in halls were staying in bed till the afternoon and going to lectures once a week for a few hours. But I didn't mind because I was doing the thing that I always wanted! I was teaching and learning how best to do it and having that opportunity to work with children in a real school felt important and like I was making a difference. Many of the schools were in disadvantaged areas and knowing that I had at least provided a safe and fun environment for a few hours made me proud.

In between my studies, I always had a weekend job and holiday job – I was a cleaner and a children's entertainer - I can rustle up a balloon dog if you really want me to! I also worked in administration, and at university I was an alumni caller, where you ring ex-students and ask for money for the university. I was pretty good at it, and we had KPI's and prizes for the highest donation, as well as a leader board (and this was something that stuck with me, even when I went into teaching.) Having that competition element really motivated me, but more to compete with myself, I wanted to always beat my amount from the week before.

I also worked at Greggs (70% off – dangerous!) and loved having that customer interaction even though my adding up left something to be desired. I was often corrected in my addition but quickly learned, and I also made a mean ham sandwich. All the sandwiches were handmade and fresh on site, and I loved that element of the job, too. The lady who managed the store (I wish I could remember her name properly but I think it might have been Barbara) was so patient and kind as I had never worked in a retail environment before (I don't include the party shop the entertainment company owned, for the time when I was a children's entertainer as no one came in and I was able to do all my GCSE revision whilst getting paid!)

I graduated in 2003, moved to Harrow with the boyfriend and committed to my first teaching job in High Wycombe. The school was in the middle of a council estate, and looking back, I was very naïve. As a somewhat sheltered 20-something, I had no idea about the levels of poverty that existed and that existed in this area. I had children in my class who rarely had new clothes, rarely washed and were desperate for my attention. Sometimes, that desperation came out as wanting to be physically close to me all the time, in others, they threw chairs, they screamed at me, and one student even ran out the classroom, across the playground and into a nearby woods. For several hours we did not know where he had gone, and to be the teacher who was in charge when that happened was a pretty devastating place to be. Looking back now, I can see that I should have had more support as a student teacher, that incident stayed with me for a long time.

After two years of being a teacher, I sadly decided I had enough. A lack of support, but a lot of "management" by a management team who weren't really interested in the children and more in the league tables, made me disillusioned with education. Who knows, if I had started my career in a different (better managed) school, I may still be doing it now. But it wasn't to be, and I decided publishing was the job for me. What I failed to research, was that publishing is a very much who you know world, or at least it was 20 years ago. I didn't know anyone who could give me a way in, and I couldn't afford to be a non-paid member of staff. Volunteering was simply not an option, with bills to contribute to and a car to run.

So, I looked at sales jobs instead. I went to several of those HORRENDOUS group interviews for advertising in publishing (I was telling myself this was just as good as working on children's books…) where they pit you against each other, give you arbitrary games to "win" against all odds and then pick a handful of candidates to try out and see if you last a week in the actual job.

I was delighted to discover that I actually was the last person standing for one role. The chap leading the charade told me I would be meeting the head of advertising. She was terrifying. We walked into her office – she had her feet up on the table, was dressed impeccably, and she simply asked me - "who are you?" as if I was the most inconsequential being on the planet or, indeed, the solar system. After what felt like years of listening to the interview chap telling her how great I was in the interview, she offered me a job. Needless to say – I didn't take it. I knew that was not the way to treat people. I said no thank you to the job and told the recruiter exactly how this woman had behaved towards me.

What next?

Not long after this incident, I got a call from, I think, (it was a long time ago now, dear reader!) the same agency asking me if I would consider interviewing to work for them as a recruiter. This option had never crossed my mind, and I didn't really understand what a recruiter did, apart from making a lot of phone calls to me, which was what I had experienced in my job search.

I went for that interview, and despite not being successful, it sparked an interest and desire to work in the recruitment industry. It ticked a lot of boxes for me – teamwork, having targets, a sales focus, but also that customer service element and dealing with people were all high priorities for me. I interviewed at several recruitment businesses (and some of the biggest names were truly awful at interviewing!) but the one that caught my attention was an international temp business. It is still going today, and I owe a great deal to what I learnt from the many great managers I had in my ten years working there.

Having been successful at interviews, I started as a recruiter, earning £15000 a year in central London. I had made it!! I loved my manager (more on her later), and even my interview with her still goes down in history for me as one of the most enjoyable of my working career. It was a conversation, it didn't really feel like a test and some of the questions sent me down some surreal scenarios which I really enjoyed. I recruited finance staff into the public sector, which then included charities and the NHS. My first placement was for a charity run by a wife and husband team who worked from home (unusual in those days!) and who decided they needed the help of a qualified accountant.

I loved it. The atmosphere, the camaraderie, and perhaps strangely -the pressure. Even now, I need a bit of pressure to get things done (including writing this! I would not lie to you!) The sales element was enough to keep me on my toes, but it felt like a subtle kind of sell. Not selling cars but selling people's skills. There is a skill and nuance to selling a person's skills that people outside the industry may not realise. For me, it was all about the art of selling, selling when no one realises it, not manipulating but simply listening with intent to what that other person wants. I train recruiters now to always listen for the things people don't say – that is just as powerful, and sometimes more so, than the things they do say. It's the space in between that you have to search out in recruitment. And that suited my brain. I was about 6/7 months into it when I identified my passion and long-term goal. That was to be a recruitment trainer. It felt perfect. Using my knowledge from teaching and transferring this to my interest in sales, in the psychology of sales and seeing people develop. This was it!

And so began the waiting game. This led to over four years of setting up new accounts, mentoring new hires, and conducting training sessions for small groups as part of my new career path. I even secured new accounts with the Home Office and the Prison Service, and consistently ranked as one of the top performers in terms of sales. My only competition was myself, as I never paid much attention to what others were doing, and I had no desire to become a manager. My goal was solely focused on obtaining that coveted training position, and I was determined to achieve it. In September 2007, my old manager, who was now the company Trainer, had a meeting with me and told me – "we need you now".

I started in my new full-time training role in January 2008, and I still remember that feeling of excitement that I had achieved what I wanted. So followed five wonderful years learning how to train, facilitate groups, writing training content, giving feedback and encouragement as well as supporting stakeholders across the country. I travelled all over the UK, which I loved, working closely with recruiters and management to ensure they were getting the results the business needed. I also took on the role of internal recruiter and coordinated interview Assessment days for the London and national offices. My manager and I were the perfect team, we often came at problems from different directions and we shared the same sense of humour.

I fell pregnant with our first child in the May of 2011, and immediately felt ill, and was ill most days for 14 weeks. Trying to travel and train whilst this was going on was challenging, but I got through it, and luckily it did subside after 14 weeks. We were on holiday in France, and I remember waking up and panicking because I felt totally normal – was I still pregnant? I was, and on the first Feb 2012, we welcomed William John Braid. I enjoyed a whole year of mat leave. In the early months, I had no idea how much I would miss working.

We didn't get much sleep with William during the early days, and there would be days and weeks where we were both living on little more than 3 hours of sleep a night. But we got through it, and after a few months, I had a bit more energy to go to the baby groups, and baby massage and all the things you felt you had to do as a parent to a new baby in South London. If I am being honest with you dear reader – I was bored. William didn't want to sing – well, he couldn't, could he. And I didn't want to sit on the floor of a cold hall with women I didn't know from Adam and, quite frankly, was too exhausted to talk to. So I stopped going. I still saw my NCT group, and we would have days out and picnics and do baby cinema (Alien – Resurrection, anyone), and that was enough for me.

And there it loomed – the day I was to return to work. The nursery we wanted William to attend only had availability for a Monday and Friday for the first six weeks. I fed this back to my director. The answer was no, sorry, we can't accommodate that. To say I was distraught was an understatement. It was only about five or so years later I realised how upset I was at being treated like this.

Ten years of service, and you can't wait six weeks? Of course, we know they just didn't want me back and didn't want to pay my salary. At this point, my wonderful manager was now herself on maternity leave, so without her, the pull to go back was a lot less. We worked so well together, so with her not there, I didn't really feel I was missing much by leaving.

A blessing in disguise?

The reality of the situation was –they did me a favour. I had already been there for ten years. Did I want to stay another ten years? I realised the answer was – no. So, I updated my CV, put it on every job board going, and waited. A few days later, I had a call from the MD of a start-up legal recruitment business. Would I be interested in interviewing for their Internal Recruitment Manager role? They were a growing business and needed someone with a recruitment background to take charge of that growth with their recruitment and interview process. I bought myself a new coat, wiped off the nappy cream and very happily got offered the job.

I had my first offer for an experienced recruiter to start three weeks into the job, and I was delighted, as were the owners of the business. Within 3.5 years, I grew that business to 24 heads; I had an office manager reporting to me and was the Director of Operations. I learnt so much from this business and from the MDs who owned it. Yes, there were stressful times, but there were also joyous and exciting times too. Growing a business requires stamina and effort, and as a management team, we understood this. Leading as a human was important to us all and still drives this business now.

A new chapter

I always wanted to run my own training business. It is important to me that my children have a mum who enjoys her work, is her own boss and is happy and fulfilled in her work life. I hope that they strive for that too- not settling but really going out there for what makes them fulfilled and happy. I know not everyone gets that privilege. I was lucky to have two parents and Grandparents who always encouraged me and honestly believed I could do whatever I chose to do.

Three and half years in at the legal business, we got to the point where they didn't need me full-time; my Office manager was much better at the facilities piece than I was (and I told her this regularly – she is now director of operations and has been for about six years) and I wasn't really being utilised in the way that suited my strengths.

This felt like an opportunity. After some soul searching and asking myself, am I ready for this? Is this the right time? I decided I wanted to set up my own training business. This might be a surprise to you, but this idea originally occurred to me during my training role in my first recruitment job. It was one of those things at the time that felt too hard, too impossible – who am I to think I can run my own business? But having a father who was entrepreneurial and a mother who made a career as a talented teacher, really the clues were there. I continued to work with the Legal business two days a week, and they became my very first client. I provided performance reviews, individual coaching, and training whilst carrying out business development to find other clients and promote my new training services. One and a bit years in, I had our daughter and only took seven months off – I was paranoid I would lose clients. I did two days a week for four months, which allowed me to get back into it without being too exhausted.

Seven years in, and I have built a business I am proud of. I still get to pick up my children and be around for the important things in their life while building a business that works for my clients and my family. I have worked with FTSE-listed businesses, start-ups, and everything in between. My reason for doing what I do is to help recruiters develop their skills so they can enjoy their work. I am as passionate about achieving that goal for my clients as I have ever been.

Recruitment can be a stressful and pressured environment, so helping recruiters develop the techniques and skills to make their life feel easier so they can enjoy what they do is my why. Life is too short not to enjoy what you do for a living. So, you might as well make it fun!

If you would like to partner with me to develop your teams, you can email me at **ali@therecruitmenttrainer.co.uk**

Or call me on 07855 868478 to explore how we can work together.
And check out my off-the-shelf courses:
www.therecruitmenttrainer.co.uk

And my online BD Essentials course:

Business Development - Essentials For Success Online Course - The Recruitment Trainer

THE RISE OF THE FEMALE ENTREPRENEUR

CHAPTER 18
Kathleen Van den Berghe
Entrepreneur in wine & tourism

More fun, less shizzle!
Laying the foundations

I was born, raised, and am still based in Belgium, and I own and manage two wine estates in the French Loire Valley. That may seem odd, but I have always been very internationally oriented. I have studied and worked in many countries and learned six languages, three of which I speak almost daily. I have a passion for studying and learning.

I am a construction engineer and have worked in construction and real estate for a total of six years. The construction industry was (and probably still is) very male-dominated and quite conservative, hence I quickly felt stuck. Construction projects also take a long time, which was testing my patience and my yearning for new challenges. So, after doing an MBA, I became a McKinsey consultant, enjoying it a lot for nine years. The projects were shorter and very intense, the intellectual challenge was enormous, I learned every day on the job and undertook extra training to further develop myself. I travelled constantly, as I worked in France, Luxembourg, Spain, Switzerland, Thailand, Greece, Cyprus and Qatar. I attended training and conferences on all continents. I was single, and I was loving it!

During those McKinsey days, I also met my future husband (also a McKinsey consultant). We got married and had our first child. Our combined rhythms were not compatible with a baby. I also discovered that I loved being a very hands-on project manager, but I didn't feel like becoming a partner. The partner role felt too conceptual and less hands-on for me. Hence, I left the "golden cage", of my job which was a painful process. Why quit a "perfect" job and career with a great salary when you weren't asked to leave (as often happened to other people)? It took me several months to make that decision, and my husband was a very good sparring partner. He was clearly well fit for the partner role, while I was very different. He supported me in all my choices, as he has continued to do since.

I took a "regular" job in real estate in Belgium, meaning in an office with office hours and commuting. That was the first and the last experience for me! To make it more interesting, I did a part-time postgraduate course in real estate.

But the commute and office-style work did not suit me at all. So, I started to consider changing my career, becoming my own boss, and managing my own business. By then I knew what I enjoyed: "creating" something (like in construction), working in an international environment, hospitality and events, and challenging projects.

Around that same period, my husband and I decided to look for a holiday home. We didn't like the seaside, nor did we like the warm South of Europe. But we both liked wine, so we looked for a holiday home in the vineyards, ideally with some vines to make our own wine on the side.

It turns out I am very efficient in "searching" and planning. The idea for a holiday home started during the Christmas 2010 holidays. During the Easter 2010 holidays, I organized a four-day trip to 3 different French wine regions with 4-5 visits per day. And in my search I had discovered that there are in fact, very nice houses with a lot more than a few vines. And the prices were very reasonable (compared to holiday homes in sunny locations). Armed with excel sheets and comparisons of the three short-listed properties, we chose the one that had appealed to us the most and had the most potential for the future. On top, it had been managed by women for over two centuries, and it was called Château de Minière ("mining castle") My husband worked in the mining industry his whole career. Too much serendipity to ignore!

The first papers were signed early July 2010, and the final papers mid September 2010, immediately followed by harvest 2010. Some people dream of a wine estate, but for me, it was a real job from day 1. The holiday home had turned into a business venture. I stopped my office job in Belgium and went full-time into the French wine industry.

I should also add that I discovered I was pregnant with our second child during this search. Simon was born in December 2010. It was a very hectic year, and that rhythm would remain for the following years.

Building a wine business

My wine journey really started in September 2010 with my first harvest in Bourgueil in France. It's funny how people seem to think that making wine is a part-time occupation... I keep getting questions like "What do you really do?", "What is your real job?" as if winemaking is limited to watching grapes grow and harvesting them. That is, of course, not true! Growing grapes takes a full year, but growing high-quality grapes takes several years as you need to improve the vineyards and the plants year on year. And winemaking takes at least six months for young wines but 2-3 years for high-end wines. And you get one chance a year to make a certain wine, so you need to learn and improve year on year. Hence making high quality wine takes decades of gradual improvement. Winemaking has really taught me patience!

I always say that Minière was a double full-time job. I had to improve the wine quality, and I have renovated the entire estate into a high-end wine tourism destination where you can visit, taste, eat, have seminars and group activities and also stay with up to 27 people in very high-end rooms with en-suite modern bathrooms. No creaky beds or leaking taps, all is new, but with the atmosphere of bygone centuries.

As a winemaker, we start from the vineyard by selecting the plants, preparing the soils, growing the grapes and improving them over many years. Then we harvest at the optimal ripeness. Making good quality wine is very technical and takes time, and then we bottle the wine, and we create and source the packaging, and only then can we start selling the wine. But sales is the main aspect of the wine business. If we do not sell a bottle, then we have no income, even though we have invested all the time and energy into making the wine. And there is no lack of good wine in the world, so we need to be very active in order to get noticed and find clients.

The start of my wine journey was really hard, as I was new into the wine business, and it turned out that Bourgueil was a very traditional wine village, hence a Belgian woman leading a wine estate and doing things differently, led to a lot of gossip, and unfriendly remarks. But it also turned out that my first team was not really adequate to make high-end wine. With hindsight, this was to be expected as such a beautiful wine estate would only be sold if there was a real problem. The wine estate was indeed bankrupt, because the wine quality was average and hence the sales price was too low to cover the costs. The quality of the people was of course, part of the problem. Furthermore, the winemaker was not trustworthy technically nor financially. I discovered that fairly quickly, but it took a lot of energy and time to uncover that and to fire him. It turned out it was not easy to hire a winemaker who was capable, loyal, and honest. But after many trials and more than ten years, I have found the right one, and she is a woman as well, maybe no surprise. It was equally difficult to build the rest of the team and find trustworthy people who do their job well, also when I am absent, but I managed to build an exceptional team who go above and beyond for our clients.

The objective at the start was that we would move with the family to France as my husband could travel from France as well, and we looked forward to a larger house with a large garden in a more gentle climate than Belgium. But first, I needed to renovate the Château, and after a few years of going back and forth, my husband discovered that travelling from rural France was difficult. In parallel, I discovered that we could rent out the Château as a holiday home (and use it ourselves as a holiday home when we wanted). We also preferred to raise our kids in our international area around Brussels rather than a small French village away from everything. Besides that, over these first years I had realized that coming home to "normal" non-wine people was very beneficial for my mental health. The pressure around the wine estate in France was really enormous and escaping that regularly has certainly prevented me from burning out.

My wine business expanded when I added white wine with the acquisition of a second wine estate in Loire, Château de Suronde, located in Quarts de Chaume Grand Cru. This is the only Grand Cru in Loire, so there is a lot of potential for high quality wine. We farm the 6ha of vineyards biodynamically, and we also have over 10ha of wild nature, which is perfect for biodiversity. The environment is super inspiring, and as I love art, I have created an artist residence there. On the wine estate, we also rent out two houses for holidays.

During all these years, I also kept on studying in order to quickly learn a lot about winemaking and wine tasting. In 2010 I started with a technical course, to understand the ins and outs of viticulture and winemaking, and every day I learn on the job from my team. After that I learned theory and tasting of wines across the world by following all the WSET (Wine & Spirit Education Trust) courses. WSET Level 4 Diploma is really difficult, with a lot of self-study on the weekends at home with small kids, but I learned a huge amount that was also very valuable for my own estates.

Then I discovered the ultimate challenge in wine: I embarked on the Master of Wine journey, the holy grail of wine education, a very challenging program.

There are only 413 Masters of Wine in the world. I am proud to say that I am now one step away from reaching that goal, and then I will be the first Belgian (even Benelux) woman to obtain that title!

Proud of the results

The first ten years of my journey were incredibly intense, combining a new sector with a lot of turnaround work and a family, spread over two countries. With hindsight, I was on autopilot, very focused on my goal. I have now achieved what I aimed to achieve, making very high-quality organic wines in different styles: three sparkling wines, white, rosé and red still wines and sweet white wines. You can pair all dishes with my wines; there is no need to look any further!

I am most proud of my red sparkling wine, Bulles de Minière rouge, which is very original and very tasty. There truly is no other wine in this style in the world. Most are either sweeter or more tannic, hence not as balanced and refreshing as mine. It is, of course, a very particular style, but wine consumers are looking for original wines with a story, and that wine certainly fits the bill!
I am also very proud of our position in wine tourism. Château de Minière is open every day for visits, tasting, meals, etc. You can do seminars and team building activities and you can of course stay at our estate with 12 rooms in a very high-end exclusive environment. This is truly unique and appeals to the clients. In Château de Suronde you can stay in smaller houses that are more modest in line with the secluded natural environment, oriented to people who want to disconnect and relax in the middle of nature.

I built on this experience and offer holiday rentals in Switzerland and in the Belgian Ardennes. I discovered I am very efficient at finding unique places in the middle of nature and renovating them to match the style to their environment and then renting them out. I always say that I sell "joy" in the form of a bottle of wine or a holiday. I sell "unforgettable memories" and unique experiences with family or friends to remember. An evening with friends and a good bottle of wine is as much of an experience as a weekend or holiday with friends or family. These are all memories that stay with you, and you keep talking about them.

I am very proud of myself and my team that we have very high ratings on all platforms for our rentals and activities. This requires a lot of work and commitment every day to give our clients unforgettable experiences.

What I have learned along the way

During my whole career I have been very interested in personal development and coaching. I have read many books and followed several trainings, including a coaching training, as I want to help other people reach their full potential and enjoy life and business to the fullest. Building on almost 30 years of business experience, I am ready to share my experience and my knowledge and help other people on their journey. Here are a few of my lessons and advice for fellow entrepreneurs.

More fun, less shizzle

This is the first and the most important one that overarches all the others. In life and in business, we have a choice of what we do, who we work with, etc. It is very important to focus on the fun and avoid the shizzle. The shizzle easily drags us down, drains our energy, uses our time, etc. And if we do not pay attention, we easily get dragged into the shizzle, e.g. by selling to non-ideal clients, working with difficult suppliers, having negative team members, etc. This can happen without noticing, but you do feel your energy draining. So, when this happens, take a moment, look around and eliminate the shizzle situations. When you need to make a decision, you can also check whether it will add fun or become shizzle. It is really a very good barometer for what to do and what to drop!

Go where energy flows

Continuing from the above, follow the positive energy, do what gives you energy, and avoid what drains your energy. This is especially important when your company grows, and you can finally hire team members to support you. As an entrepreneur you should focus on your strengths, what makes your business what it is, what makes you unique, and also what gives you energy. You should delegate what is draining your energy (but needs to be done), what takes you more time than someone else, etc. These choices are very personal and can also change over time.

Clarify your values

Both in McKinsey and in my real estate job, I discovered the benefits of having explicit values, hence I determined the values of my own company very early on and shared them with my team and all new people that join my company. Values can guide everyday behaviour. E.g. My first value is "client first", so when a client enters our estate or calls, the team knows that this takes priority over everything else, including finishing whatever they were doing at that moment. It is also easier to evaluate people on values than on actions. For example, when a team member makes a mistake, you can check whether it was a case of lacking experience or knowledge or a case of bad will. Everybody makes mistakes, but when you know the real cause, it is easier to take the appropriate actions.

Dance close to the revenue line

As an entrepreneur you always have a zillion things on your to do list, and the "getting things done" approach is not always very helpful as you end up wasting time organizing your to do's.... An alternative way is to think of all your to-do's related to an income statement: do they bring revenue, do they add costs, do they add investments, etc? In case you are overwhelmed, it helps to prioritize those actions that will help you bring in revenue, either by bringing in new clients, making invoices or making clients pay their bills. Or maybe building a new website to attract new clients. Those actions should take priority over back-office actions or peripheral actions. This helps to create clarity, especially when overwhelmed.

Be yourself, the rest is already taken

As a newcomer into an existing industry, we often suffer from imposter syndrome. We feel different, with less experience, and we feel judged, like I did in the wine industry. But I discovered that the world needs different people, as all clients are also different looking for different suppliers. So, in the end, being different is a competitive advantage as you attract your clients with their specific needs who are not well served by the existing offer. Make it a strength to be different, advertise your differences and attract your specific audience. Be proud to be different and realize that everything is possible! There are no limits; if you can imagine it, you can do it.

FAIL = First Attempt in Learning!

Do not see failure or mistakes as a problem and as a reason to stop but learn from them to improve and to move on. On the contrary, if you do not try new things, you will never know if it works. And that may just be your competitive advantage: to be different from the others. I believe a lot in trying new things on a small scale, getting feedback quickly and learning from it. Then, either improve and try a better version next time or stop the project. Also, if you try new things, you can offer them for free in exchange for feedback and/or a review for your business. In any case, every trial is useful and brings you closer to your goal!

It helps to consider that everything has already been done or tried before, but maybe not in your business or with your specific combination. So, you can go faster by learning from other people's trials and mistakes or successes and adapt to your context. It is just a matter of finding who already did what and identify what you can learn from them.

Less pressure, more pleasure

In the end, it is all about how much pressure we put on ourselves, based on what we expect for ourselves, what we need to do, and how we need to do it. Which and especially whose expectations do we want to conform to?

Many female entrepreneurs have too many balls in the air and aim for perfection in many different fields at the same time: business, friends, health, partner, children, parents, ...

It is useful to evaluate what you really want for yourself and why you do certain things. Does it really add value, give you joy, make you smile, bring you pleasure? Or is there an external pressure at work, explicitly (e.g. what your parents tell you) or implicitly (e.g. something you have learned as a child)?

If you focus on what brings YOU joy, it will be easier to follow your own path with less pressure and more pleasure!
Don't forget: More fun, less shizzle!
Interested to learn more about me and my journey?

I give talks about my entrepreneurial journey, in person and digital, with and without wine. I really enjoy sharing my story and my lessons learned in order to inspire others!

Feel free to contact me!
LinkedIn: www.linkedin.com/in/kathleenvandenberghe
Facebook: https://www.facebook.com/kathleenvdberghe/
Instagram https://www.instagram.com/kathleenvandenberghe/

All my activities are here:
Website: www.kathleenvandenberghe.com

Visit us for a wine tasting and/or a holiday or order wine at home:
Website: www.chateaudeminiere.com
Website: www.chateaudesuronde.com

CHAPTER 19
Kaytie Chambers
The Aesthetics Growth Coach

My name is Kaytie, and I went from being £10k in debt, working 12 hour days and never seeing my children, to working half the hours and earning £10k per month as an Aesthetics Nurse. I did this by creating a framework that ensures a steady flow of clients and revenue, sparing me from the daunting task of starting from zero each month. Now, I want to share my expertise and help as many female aesthetic practitioners as possible to reclaim their freedom and build a business around their life, not the other way round.

The transition into Aesthetics was the easy part, the realm where science meets art, and beauty was right up my street, recognised as a naturally gifted injector,

I was chosen as one of the UK's top emerging injectors, and my company has earned multiple awards. The challenges were navigating the business side, particularly sales, didn't come easily at first! It took time, but I crafted a system that consistently brought in clients throughout the year, relieving a lot of the pressure as a business owner, and now I teach other service-based business owners to do the same thing.

It hasn't been an easy path. Along the way, I faced a few challenges, you see, beneath the surface of flawless faces and enviable skin, harbours hustle cultures, egos, jealousy, and cutthroat competition. I even hit rock bottom and nearly gave up everything, but you know what they say about rock bottom, right? The only way is up...

I put people in the freezer

My journey hasn't exactly been a walk in the park. I used to be the kind of person who'd rather dodge social media because the idea of being judged made me squirm. It kept me on the side-lines for years. And money talk? Oh, that was like a cringe-worthy dance of discomfort every time I asked somebody to pay me. Long story short, I didn't recognise the true worth of my skills or time.

Consequently, I found myself practically giving things away daily, mainly treating friends and completely winging it on social media. Naively, I believed that merely sharing what I was doing and showcasing my before and afters would fill my schedule effortlessly. Granted, I was making enough to cover bills, but being "Businesswoman of the Year" felt far off, and a year later, I was steering a company without any previous acumen, operating without a plan.

By this time, I had left the NHS for hopes of working less and earning more. I had visions of spending the weekends and holidays with my young family, yet I found myself putting in more hours than I ever did in the NHS. Unsurprisingly, I found myself entangled in cortisol's grip, constantly comparing myself to others, never feeling good enough and hurtling toward the brink of a possible mental breakdown or business failure.

As I struggled to stay afloat, jealousy became an extra hurdle as three local practitioners decided to sabotage my business and tarnish my character individually. Things escalated when they teamed up. At that point, I wasn't mentally strong enough to ignore them. My confidence was low, and I was grappling with postnatal depression. It was easy to get caught up in their games and let their negativity overshadow the little light there was left. Then, with a mere flicker left, the universe decided to hurl me yet another curveball; this time, it had "FU" scrawled all over it!

In March 2020, my business took an unexpected break. Back then, it felt like the worst thing imaginable, and it was like the universe was screaming GIVE UP! I started to embrace that negative mindset even more. Lockdown brought some dark times, presenting a business challenge and a personal one. Faced with this double challenge, I had two options: sink or swim (thankfully, I chose to swim). It was a strange and scary time, but it allowed people to slow down and to appreciate the smaller things in life that mean the most. It allowed people to evaluate their life, to look inwards and to truly understand what was valuable to them, and for me, it was my family. I just wanted to feel more confident, be less anxious and spend as much time as possible with the kids because they were growing up so fast.

Looking back now, lockdown wasn't a signal to quit; it was an opportunity to grow. The main source of my issues was my own negative thinking—constantly feeling inadequate as a mother and business owner, it was a never-ending cycle. However, being confined made me confront my demons, marking the beginning of my personal growth journey.

During the many, many walks in lockdown, I started to tune into self-help podcasts. It dawned on me that to succeed in both life and business, I needed to adopt a completely new way of thinking. This realisation was a turning point. I discovered that unlocking success in the aesthetics industry required more than just strategic execution; it demanded a profound shift in mindset. Without addressing and unblocking the mental barriers, I would remain tethered to a cycle of stagnation and self-sabotage. It was time to bid farewell to self-doubt and anxiety and start living the life I wanted. Little did I know, this newfound mindset would transform my life and pave the way for me to help other aesthetic practitioners break free from their mental barriers too. As for the haters? I put them in the freezer! Don't worry, not literally, of course; that would be weird. It's just a cool mindset hack I use to shake off negativity.

Here's the quick rundown: Take 5-10 minutes to chill out, think about what these people did, write down their names on a piece of paper, stick it in a jar of water, and freeze it. So, when thoughts of them or their negativity try to creep back in, just remind yourself, "Nope, they're in the freezer." It's a simple way to remember that you've cut them out and won't waste any more energy on them.

Mother-hustler

In addition to freezing people, I needed something more substantial to break free from the negative spiral and victim mode I was sitting in; a shift in mindset was crucial. First, I started to follow inspirational, uplifting and empowering content online. I continued listening to powerful podcasts, and I increased my exercise activity. Slowly I began to adopt a growth mindset and reframed "Why is everything bad happening?" to "Everything happens for me, not to me." I started to view every curveball the universe threw at me (though not always pleasant) as an opportunity for growth rather than a setback and rather than dwelling on the past. As I adopted a more abundant mindset, I saw more silver linings, and I was able to respond differently to the haters (yes, I added more people to the freezer). I started to take criticism better, implemented new strategies and no longer felt the need to compare myself to other Aesthetic Practitioners as much. The impact of this mindset shift was profound, reflected in the multiple awards and the establishment of a six-figure company since the business reopened after lockdown.

My business boomed, and the clients rolled in like I never imagined. However, it wasn't long before I dropped into old habits and started to become addicted to the hustle again. Before I knew it, I was working all day every day again. The realisation came when my little boy asked me to look at him playing, but I was so focused and absorbed in writing the perfect social media caption I unintentionally growled, "In a minute, I'm working", and his disappointed face broke my heart. Something similar happened again that week when I chose work over the cinema with my family, my daughters' words, "You're always working", echoed in my ears, and that's when it hit me.

My bounce back era was going well on paper, but at the cost of everything I cherished. Ironically, I chose this career to create more time with my loved ones, yet there I was, allowing my business to consume me, isolating myself and addicted to the hustle culture, which was a far cry from the family focused freedom I set out to achieve. Despite handling stress better, I found myself caught in constant busyness, unwittingly on a journey to Burnout City and potentially, divorce! You see, the hustle culture modernises hard work and long hours as the key to success, but often at the cost of things that really matter, like your well-being and family. Fuelled by a relentless drive for perfection and success, business owners may find themselves working tirelessly, convinced that constant busyness equates to progress. I'm here to tell you that it's nonsense. Succumbing to this culture not only jeopardises your mental health but also depletes your creative energy, fostering a toxic environment. If you resonate with this uneven work life balance and you want to carve a pathway from overwhelm to freedom, I have good news for you. It's achievable; you can shape a business around your life rather than the other way around. The first step is to identify what truly matters and reconnect with your purpose, that's what I did.

Often, people shape their lives around their businesses, sacrificing moments with their children or working late nights because they believe it's necessary for success. However, a better strategy is to build a business that fits into your life. During lockdown, I realised that my happiness comes from family time and a balanced work life, but I had lost sight of this. I needed to reconnect with my purpose so that I could create stronger boundaries and start to build the life that I wanted, not the one that I was constantly being sucked into. One of the interventions I love to do is the best possible self-exercise; you can download it at **www.aestheticsgrowthcoach.com**

Now that I had reconnected with my purpose, I set both long-term and short-term goals. I refer to goal setting as like our GPS for turning dreams into reality. It's about picturing the future we want and breaking it into doable steps. To establish a clear path for success, an effective approach is to set SMART goals: Specific, Measurable, Achievable, Relevant, and Time-bound. Goal setting isn't rigid; it's a flexible process that brings clarity, purpose and growth that guides you towards personal and professional success. But it's important to remember, it's not just about just racing to the end goal; the journey matters too. Celebrating small wins along the way will keep you motivated and on track.

Circles are boring

To start my journey toward freedom, I did something a little crazy. I got rid of half of my services. I wanted to reduce the feeling of overwhelm so I decided to get rid of anything on my treatment menu that didn't bring me joy, dialling in on my strengths and keeping activities where I was in flow. If you're not familiar with the concept of flow, it's where you're doing an activity, and time feels like it has sped up. You might have heard people say, 'get into the flow.' It's a bit like mindfulness, where you're fully absorbed, concentrated, and enjoying what you're doing. Being in this positive state can make you happier, more energised, and motivated. Tapping into this was going to be my secret weapon.

In the hustle culture days, I attempted to be a jack-of-all-trades, offering a variety of services—from lip fillers to fat dissolving, peels to mole removal, you name it, I did it. Honestly, I wasn't great at everything, and I didn't even enjoy many of the treatments, especially fat dissolving! I provided them just because other practitioners did, and unknowingly, I ended up evolving into this circle. As children, we're often taught to be well-rounded, like circles, by strengthening our weaknesses. Think about school—say you struggled with maths but excelled in French. Typically, you'd get a maths tutor, becoming mediocre in both subjects. But what if you had a French tutor and excelled in that?

Allow me to explain further. Imagine a star – it has dips (representing weaknesses) and points (representing strengths). The more you focus on nurturing these, the more they thrive. Many invest time in developing weaknesses, creating a well-rounded circle. Yet, let's face it, circles can be a bit dull. Now, picture concentrating on cultivating and elevating strengths, the points of the star. As you nurture them, they extend longer, creating a superstar.

On my quest to become a superstar, I also honed in and learned more about my niche. The better you know your ideal client, the more you can fine-tune your messaging and talk to them directly. It's a smart move that can really change the game for your business, which became apparent as I embraced a strength-based approach. My diary started to fill up, but the workload was exhausting. Juggling roles as the Aesthetics Nurse, social media manager, email marketer, and lead generator became overwhelming, and the constant hunt for clients was draining me. I was grateful but very, very busy.

All these factors were once again pulling me away from my goal of freedom. I remember being sat in my kitchen, feeling completely overwhelmed by the tasks I had in front of me, desperate to get them all finished before I picked the kids up from school so that my work didn't eat into family time. And I just remember thinking, there's got to be a simpler way, aesthetics shouldn't be this demanding. That's when I decided to create something unique, a system that generates consistent clients without starting from scratch each month—something that would profoundly transform both my business and my life.

The Recurring Revenue Engine!

During that week, I came up with a sure-fire system that schedules my appointments six months ahead, taking away the hassle of chasing clients, constantly selling on social media, and the overall pressures of running an aesthetics business. This system not only eased the stress but also helped future-proof my business. While others in the aesthetics field might face slowdowns in the summer and January, I maintain a steady flow of clients. I developed a subscription model that would completely change the trajectory of my business, for the better.

A subscription works a bit like a gym membership, but for your face. Clients pay monthly and come in every five weeks to experience aesthetic or skin services. The clients love this arrangement because they enjoy high-end treatments at membership prices, and you will love it because it maintains a steady flow of clients, and you can earn an extra £3-5k recurring revenue every single month. But it goes beyond that – introducing a subscription-based service has a profound ripple effect on your entire business. It builds a sense of community and creates a database of ideal clients who trust you. As a result, they not only engage in other services but also become valuable advocates for your aesthetics business, recommending it to others.

The subscription system I've developed is a game-changer for aesthetics businesses. Despite attempts by others to copy (even those practitioners I mentioned earlier, and yes, they're still in the freezer), many fall short and end up with memberships that flop. While imitation is considered flattering, why leave it to chance when I can provide you with the blueprint to creating, selling, and managing a client subscription model in your Aesthetics, Skin & Laser Business. This ensures a steady flow of revenue every month, sparing you from the daunting task of starting from zero each time and creating freedom within your business!

In **'The Aesthetics Growth Circle'** I teach my proven framework and the exact steps I took to build a subscription that brings in £4-5k per month with ease. When implemented correctly, it becomes the powerhouse propelling your business to skyrocket!

Just DM me the word 'SUPERSTAR', and I'll show you how!

You can connect with me on
TikTok: @TheAestheticsGrowthCoach
Instagram: @Myla_Aesthetics

CHAPTER 20
Alvina Menzies
Business Mentor & Success Activation Coach®

Rewinding my mind

Alarm. Shower. Coffee. Commute. Alarm. Shower. Coffee. Commute. Alarm. Shower. Coffee. Commute. Car broke down. Vulnerable. Afraid. Crying. Frozen.

It's dark, cold, and snowy outside, a typical February morning in Scotland. It's 1994, 7.30am and it was week one of my first full time 'proper' job as an administrator in a financial services company. £8,000 a year imagine that, feeling like the bee's knees! I was so proud of myself, hair done, make-up on (think Kylie Minogue perm and Heather Shimmer lipstick), a new blouse, skirt suit and heels. This was my third day, and I was getting used to this new grown-up routine, knowing exciting times were ahead! 5 minutes later I am standing, shivering with new shoes soaked through and covered in slush, my feet were numb, and I was knocking on a stranger's door. I felt vulnerable and stupid, not knowing what to do, having abandoned my car down the road. Shaking, feeling sad, panicky, and crying like a baby. All because my wee blue Metro, my college comrade of 3 years had decided to give up and didn't want to go to work anymore.

Meanwhile, my mind was frantic with worry. What would my boss say? Would I get in trouble for being late? Would I lose my job? How will I get to work now I've no car? What about my hair, I can't go in with it soaking wet? My shoes…I need dry shoes, dry clothes. They'll be talking about me. They'll laugh at me. I've let them down, I'm not good enough. Who did I think I was anyway? I don't trust myself; how could they trust me?
The seeds of self-doubt were planted.

To give you a sense of the working environment at that time - the boardroom walls were covered in portraits of the male leaders of the business reflecting the history and beginnings of their own entrepreneurial journey to success. It's hard to believe that it was about a year on from the 'crying in the snow incident' that the dress code was changed. We were allowed to wear trousers to work, how exciting! Forget at our peril though, trousers could only be worn if they were part of a suit.

The whole administration team of about 20 people at the time were 95% female, the leadership 95% male. The stock exchange daily official lists of share prices were delivered to the mailroom and filed in the dark, cold, spooky basement. The window overlooked an ancient graveyard – how's that for a metaphor looking back now? The long-standing keeper of these lists also kept safe the original handwritten Shareholder Ledger for the two investment trusts, later transferred onto BBC computers. Yes, now I do feel old!

Anyway, back to my Metro moment. This feeling of vulnerability was the moment I knew it was time to put my big girl pants on, get out there and be the best I could possibly be. This was the beginning of 22 years with this company. Back to business. Alarm. Shower. Coffee. Commute. Alarm. Shower. Coffee. Commute. Alarm. Shower. Coffee. Commute. Learn. Work hard. Recognition. Promotion. Change. Learn. Work hard. Recognition. Promotion. Change. Learn. Work hard. Recognition. Promotion.

This is the life. This is what is expected of me. I've made it. Then the real learning began.

The 24 year Yomp

"To Yomp is to trek over extended distances, with a heavy load. A strenuous and sustained trek over difficult terrain."

In 2011, together with a team of colleagues we trained and completed 'The Cateran Yomp', a nonstop hike over the Scottish wilderness, through the Cairngorm Mountains covering 52 miles over 24 hours. Completing this challenge was a significant achievement, fuelled by teamwork, ambition, and sheer determination (I am a stubborn goat after all - Capricorn sun!). It started off with high energy and excitement, little did we know we were about to experience EVERY single human emotion possible.

Genuine physical and mental exhaustion. Every single step boosted by the strength of camaraderie, community, and connections. Giving back to communities through charitable work and challenges is so important to me and this was absolutely the most humbling experience of my life. The inner courage, strength, and resilience of every single one of the amazing humans who were participating from all walks of life. It was such a privilege to walk alongside them.

Most of the time, I absolutely loved my job, the learning and sharing my knowledge. Creating and leading teams, processes, and procedures. One of the most fulfilling parts was helping people develop, succeed, and create positive, people focused cultures. Success was a bonus, recognition for working hard, gaining a promotion and more money. But I didn't do it all for me. My 'purpose' was to support my family, allowing us to have a lovely home, nice cars (too many – must have been the Metro breakdown trauma) and travel the world – a lot – we were living life to the fullest. Just as well, we didn't know what lay ahead of us.

Looking confident and super successful to the outside world, deep inside I was going through cycles where I would crumble but outwardly keep a brave face. Throughout the years experiencing periods of weeks and months signed off with stress, anxiety, and depression. Hiding under the duvet to escape the world. A cycle that I didn't realise I had the inner power to change. One night, working late on a project (again), with a colleague I physically and literally 'FELL ill' in the toilet.

Another time, feeling so exhausted, low, and stressed that when invited into an important executive meeting to give an update, I couldn't even speak one word without feeling like I was going to burst out crying, so had to leave, go home and rest. Then, there was that one Saturday doing overtime to get an important project over the line (AGAIN). It was September 2015 and the day I got a call that was going to change my life and my priorities, completely and forever. My husband was ill and on the way to hospital with a suspected kidney stone.

So many questions asked and so many lessons learned. Who can you really trust? Who genuinely cares? Who is being selfish, out only for themselves? Who has the most qualifications? Who thinks they know best? Do I care too much? Not enough? What's more important, IQ or EQ? Do they really like me? Do I deserve these promotions? Did I do something wrong? Am I working hard enough? Am I good enough? I don't have time for this. I can't do this anymore. The seeds of self-doubt were sprouting.

In my mind, the only option I had at these times was to give in, I didn't want to go to work anymore. So, guess what I told myself? I wasn't cut out for this. I wasn't good enough. Don't get me wrong, there were good times, great times, difficult times, exhilarating times, exhausting times and many, many proud times. This was the Corporate Yomp I signed up for, but I was hurtling fast down the mountain, I just didn't know it yet.

SLOW DOWN before you fall down

Who remembers the knickerbocker glory? STOP. Hold that vision. Hold that thought. Didn't they look and taste amazing? Layers upon layers, upon layers, upon layers, upon layers. It was October 2018 and here I was, 520 miles and 8 hours away from home. Sitting on the pebbly beach of Brighton, eyes closed, trying to enjoy the warmth of the late evening sun on my face, trying so hard to visualise being on a sunny beach enjoying that sweet knickerbocker glory.

Numb bum, the cold breeze on my cheeks and taste of sea spray on my lips, a stark reminder of my true reality. My mind was trying so desperately to slow down but, in that moment, I remember it feeling like a huge mish mash of sticky layers upon sticky layers of questions, thoughts, worries and fears. Not knowing what was coming next, who to trust or how I was going to make it through the next few months without completely keeling over. My 24-year corporate Yomp was over and I felt completely STUCK.

Exhausted and vulnerable, not only from a professional perspective my personal life had also been a little bit of a challenge at that time. After my husband was diagnosed with stage 4 kidney cancer in 2015 (it wasn't a kidney stone after all) my dad passed away in 2016 with lung cancer, which he never even knew about after a long battle with early onset, fronto-temporal dementia. The universe had decided even that wasn't enough, in that very same week my husband was told that his cancer had spread to his brain and needed to start radiotherapy immediately.

My two children, 13 and 11 at that time needed me nearer home. My husband needed me, but I wasn't there, I was the career woman and main earner. The layers of doubt, guilt, grief, and sadness accumulated fast. I'd let them down. I'm not good enough. Who did I think I was anyway? I shouldn't have worked so hard. I'll have to give in. I didn't want to go to work anymore. I wasn't cut out for this. I wasn't good enough. The seeds of self-doubt were growing.

I needed to slow down so I went to my favourite spot on the beach. I needed clarity, I needed to get unstuck. Sitting there, listening to the waves, wishing they would carry away all my worries, fears, and tears. Knowing deep down that there must be a solution out there for me, but what was it? That was the big question. I was so overwhelmed I couldn't think straight. What should I do? How will we cope financially if I don't work? Why is this happening to us? So many questions.

Feeling exhausted, frustrated and in the worst mental state I had ever been in my life. Pondering. Reflecting. Had this all been worth it? Working all the hours, giving so much of my time, my energy. Was my loyalty in the right or wrong places, and at what cost? All these questions stuck in my mind, and I had absolutely no idea these were also being stored and suppressed into my body's energy system.

That day on the beach I made a courageous life changing decision to leave the Corporate Yomp.

6 years have passed, and I look back at my journal from that very day. On page one it says - 'Write what should not be forgotten'. Talk about the power of manifestation and trust in the universe? I was forced to slow down, take time for myself, and guided to activate my personal power by asking one very important question.

Who am I?

6 Steps to SUCCESS - The SPRING Solution™

Over the last 30 years, I have learned so much both personally and professionally. My passion is to share this knowledge in a way that my clients feel truly supported, helping them to feel calm, confident, resilient, and ultimately successful in all aspects of life. Humans are complex beings, and we have quite a few layers to keep balanced day to day. The conscious mind, an inner energetic flow, a subconscious mind, a physical body and a spiritual (soulful) self, none of these are more important than the other, a balanced combination is key.

In every situation, you always have a choice to make and if you choose not to slow down long enough to notice, heal and nurture all these elements of 'You', any imbalance is highly likely to restrict your confidence, overall wellbeing, and your ability to be hugely successful in both your personal and professional life.

All is quiet, it's 3am, everyone is asleep and I'm sitting at my desk with pen, paper, post it notes… loads and loads of post it notes! A frequent occurrence in the first few months of 2019 which has since become a successful creative habit for me. If I wake up inspired in the middle of the night, I write down all my visions and ideas and then go back to sleep. If this sounds familiar, try keeping a notebook by your bed, write down your thoughts and get them out of your head. Scribble, draw mind maps, whatever works best for you.

You might not realise it, but this is creating your own success from your inner knowing. This is how The 6 Steps to SUCCESS and The SPRING Solution™ was born, a perfect way to gather and share all my knowledge, tips, and techniques.

One of the very first self-coaching exercises is to reflect on **'Who am I?'**. I was no longer employed, what else did I know? What was I going to do for money? **What am I responsible for? What am I afraid of? What do I enjoy doing? What do I not enjoy doing?** A few things came up for me at that time; I was a wife, a mum, an adventurous soul who loves a challenge, spontaneous, a leader of change, inspiring others to become their best self, happiest when seeing others succeed. A quick learner and an effective trainer.

What I learned most from this exercise was that I loved to **learn, help people succeed and wanted to continue giving back to my local community.**

Using The SPRING Solution™, 6 Steps to SUCCESS framework as a guide, having walked through each step myself, I now help clients learn how to slow down, in a way that works for them. I help them learn and understand new ways to improve their confidence and incorporate everything I have learned and embodied. I share endless tips and techniques to activate inner strength and personal power. The framework covers five themes of mindfulness, mental health, mindset, morale, motivation, and mentoring. I have worked with senior leaders, entrepreneurs, and business owners who as a result, have not only succeeded in their goals but continue to thrive in life and in business without the self-imposed limitations that were holding them back.

Take a moment to pause, consider what these 6 steps to SUCCESS feel like for you:

Step 1- **Slow**. Step 2 -**Pause**. Step 3 -**Revive**. Step 4 - **Inspire**. Step 5 - **Nurture**. Step 6 - **Guide**.

The transformation happens when you are ready to remove mind, energetic and subconscious blocks to your own success at the root cause, completely and forever. I'll always encourage you to lean into and trust your intuition, creating your own success.

When you work with me, any weeds that have been growing from self-doubt, negative thoughts or limiting beliefs planted in your past that have been keeping you stuck, will be gently released, and removed completely and forever, allowing space for you to grow your confidence and THRIVE.

A few other insights and tips from my own entrepreneurial journey that I would like to share with you to inspire you and set you up for success; be open minded to new ideas and opportunities, learn continuously & embody what you learn. Connect often and spend time with like minded, successful people. Share your knowledge without expectation because I truly believe that this comes back to you over time. Always show gratitude, compassion, and kindness. Also, try to remember that when you are faced with difficult challenges, you don't need to do it alone, there is always a solution, sometimes you must be brave and ask for help to find it.

Where do you see yourself 5 years from now?

In Numerology the number 5 is deeply rooted in nature and spirituality, speaks to the heart of human existence, urging introspection and growth. Halfway through the 9-year cycle.

Sitting on my bed with my laptop on my knee, writing my story at 5.25am on my 50th birthday, I can't help but notice all the 5's around me. 5 senses, 5 elements, 5 coaching modules, 5 years of learning, embodiment, and growth. Sharing my story and my own successes with you has given me the opportunity to reflect on the last 5 years of my personal and professional growth, building self-care practices, confidence, and resilience against a background of challenging life experiences. I share these all with you now to inspire you with HOPE and PASSION to help you achieve your own SUCCESS, whatever that looks like for you.

In **2019** - I set up my first business as a coach and business mentor. I opened a Health & Wellbeing Hub called Enlighten, to support mental health in the heart of my local community, providing access to subsidised coaching and holistic healing for those who could not afford these services. I trained in energy healing with Silent Counselling (Rapid Energy Release) & Reiki, together with Emotional CPR (eCPR) a life changing, compassionate 'way of being' to support individuals through trauma.

In 2020 - I had to pivot my business like many others to support our community online & stepped in to lead and manage a Social Entrepreneur Academy for 8 months, transforming their offering with online access.

31st March 2021 - The day my life changed forever. My husband of 20 years and soul mate passed away. I experienced my first real spiritual experience through Reiki healing, now that is a whole other book!

In 2022 – I set up my second business - 58 Bonnygate, a Coworking and Community Hub in the heart of my local community which has taught me so many new lessons. An intuitive decision made from my soul, again part of that other story! I trained as an eCPR & Silent Counselling trainer to cascade these amazing techniques across the world.

Continuously investing in myself, I also trained that year as a Subconscious Healing Therapy Practitioner® incorporating Inner Child therapy, Hypnotherapy practitioner, Success Activation Coach® and Energetic Activation Method, which is a powerful combination of energy healing and Human Design, activating your inner power by aligning to your energetic blueprint.

2023 – I supported many clients to transform their lives completely and forever through my VIP coaching and mentoring programme. I also supported over 50 female small business owners to start and build their businesses through 58

Bonnygate Community. To meet our social impact goals we also partnered with a local charity to provide wellbeing services from the hub to local families affected by childhood cancer and leukaemia and have fundraised over £6k for them so far.

Personally, it felt like I was in a waiting room in 2023, not exactly sure where the universe was taking me next. Another profound life changing event as I became 'Granny Alv' in October. I set up my third company Menzies Property Sourcing & Development, ready to launch for 2024. Making the complex simple, creating property solutions for your every need and freedom, wealth, and a legacy for my family for years to come.

The 5 beliefs that were my own subconscious healing recodes in 2022 have and continue to drive me for the next 5 years and beyond: **You are good enough. You are not alone. You can trust yourself. You are courageous. You are wildly successful.**

Reflecting as I write this chapter the power of working on your mindset, taking it from scarcity to abundance can bring unlimited opportunities and success. I talk about being 'burned out' as I left the corporate world, but I am also very grateful for the experiences and successes this brought me and proud of myself for reaching the 'expected' career level that I had hoped for way back in 1994 when I started out as an administrator.

2024 -2028 – My intentions are set to grow my businesses, becoming a published author and a few more plans are being hatched too! I will continue to surrender, trust the process, and allow my intuition to guide me. What guidance would I give 20-year-old Alvina standing out cold in the snow, thinking she wasn't good enough? Take one step at a time, learn as you go, be humble, be courageous. You are successful.

"Learning to SLOW down, in a way that works for you, is the most important step you can take to help you thrive both in life & in business."

I love nothing more than supporting women in business to align with their soul, goals and aspirations and have some free resources for you on my website, to help you on your own path to success.

I love to connect with like minded and like-hearted souls too, just follow the link: **https://linktr.ee/alvinamenziescoach**

THE RISE OF THE FEMALE ENTREPRENEUR

CHAPTER 21
Kate Gerald

C.E.O. of K.A.G. Recruitment Consultancy
Award Winning Founder & C.E.O. 🏆 - Entrepreneur -
Exclusive Recruitment Specialist - Coaches, Consults
and Connects - Champion of Women in Business

Recruitment Reborn: Navigating Through Change

Every career is a story, and mine is a testament to the power of resilience and innovation in the ever-evolving world of recruitment.

My journey over the last 25 years has been anything but ordinary. As I've navigated through a myriad of opportunities, candidates, clients, and unexpected twists, each day has brought its unique set of challenges and triumphs. The recruitment industry has been both my battlefield and my playground, teaching me the values of persistence, adaptability, and deviation.

When I first stepped into the world of recruitment, it was a different era. The excitement of connecting people and possibilities was palpable in every interaction. Over the years, as the industry evolved, so did I. I learned to embrace new technologies, adapt to changing markets, and anticipate the needs of both companies and candidates. This adaptability has not only been a professional necessity but a personal ethos, guiding me through the industry's ups and downs.

The experiences of redundancy, a relatively common yet challenging aspect of any career, hit me hard and made me question my choices. Facing it multiple times didn't make it any easier, but it did instil in me a resilience I hadn't previously recognised. These periods of uncertainty were challenging, yet they forced me to re-evaluate my direction and ultimately led me to one of the most rewarding decisions of my life: starting my own business…

Embarking on the entrepreneurial jaunt wasn't a walk in the park. It was fraught with long hours, tough decisions, and constant learning. It was also liberating and exhilarating. Every day, I had the opportunity to shape my destiny, make a tangible impact, and witness the direct results of my hard work. Building a business from the ground up has been one of my most formidable yet rewarding experiences.

My aim has always been to bring a personal touch to the professional world of recruitment. I've strived to grow relationships built on trust, understanding, and mutual respect. It's these connections that have made my career so fulfilling.

Seeing individuals grow and companies flourish, knowing I played a part in that process, has been incredibly satisfying.

Now, as I look back over the quarter-century of experiences, I see a mosaic of faces, places, and moments that have shaped who I am today. The excitement of the industry's diversity remains, but it's the depth of the relationships and the impact of the work that continues to drive me. The hardships, including the redundancies, were indeed challenging, but they were also transformative, providing opportunities for growth and renewal.

Building Blocks: Crafting the K.A.G. Enterprise

Launching my business felt like setting sail into uncharted waters. It was a time brimming with both excitement for what was to come and a healthy dose of nerves about the unknown. Those initial days were about rolling up my sleeves and diving into the nitty-gritty of setting up—from the thrill of choosing a business name to the practicalities of budgets and workspaces. I lived and breathed my business, cherishing every small win and learning quickly from the inevitable hiccups.

Hard work wasn't just an expectation; it was a necessity. I found myself delving into every aspect of the business, from client relations to the intricacies of marketing. It wasn't just about putting in the hours but pouring heart and soul into every task, ensuring that each decision, no matter how small, was a step towards distinction and excellence. I continuously adapted both alongside and beyond the industry with a keen eye on emerging trends and client needs. Standing out meant not only offering top-notch services, but also building a brand that resonated with trust and quality.

Yet, for all the excitement, running a business brought its fair share of personal challenges. There were moments of solitude, confronting the weight of decisions and the future of the venture resting squarely on my shoulders. The constant juggle between professional demands and personal commitments often seemed like a high-wire act. Financial pressures, client negotiations, continuously having to prove my worth, and the relentless pursuit of growth can indeed keep one awake at night.

Among the multifaceted challenges I faced, one particularly stood out: the ongoing task of valuing my worth and justifying my ability to deliver exceptional results to clients, all while operating from home without the traditional support of a team. This wasn't just a matter of navigating logistical hurdles; it was about challenging and overcoming preconceived notions about what a successful business model looks like. But with each hurdle crossed, and every goal achieved, it offered a sense of accomplishment and learning that's hard to find elsewhere.

In the early days, I learned the true essence of being a business owner—having a vision and perseverance, but it's also about vulnerability and strength. It's a role that demands not just a sharp business acumen but also a generous dose of humanity. The experience has been humbling and empowering, teaching me lessons in leadership, empathy, and resilience.

The biggest change I've perceived is in what people now say to me when I tell them I started my own business. It has evolved from "How will you have the ability to support our business working from home?" to now, "It's ok for you, you have your own business, and you can have whatever holidays you want." Within those changes of language, I can now fully see my success and how I've not only transformed my own mind into believing in myself, but others as well.

Then came a pivotal moment three years in—the outbreak of COVID-19. Just when I had found my stride, the pandemic forced a dramatic pause and reshuffle of our operations. However, our existing home-based setup proved to be an unforeseen advantage. As other businesses scrambled to adapt to remote working, we were already there. This seamless transition during such a tumultuous time not only maintained but enhanced our service delivery. Our clients valued our stability and adaptability in a time when everything else seemed uncertain. This period, challenging as it was, affirmed the resilience and flexibility of the business model we had created.

Looking back, I wouldn't trade those initial, challenging days for anything. They were the building blocks of not just my business but my character and approach to life. They helped shape a life that's been as rewarding personally as it has been professionally, filled with growth, learning, and an ever-present drive to do better.

Building a Legacy: The K.A.G. Way

My purpose has always been clear: to do things differently. From the outset, I wanted to disrupt the norm, challenge the status quo, and introduce a more nuanced, personal approach to the recruitment process. This industry isn't just about matching resumes with job descriptions; it's about understanding the aspirations and personalities of each candidate and the culture and needs of each client.

My path wasn't paved with the typical accolades of academic excellence. School was a challenge, and my performance was often underwhelming in the traditional sense. I remember vividly the voices of doubt, especially one teacher who believed I wouldn't amount to much due to my academic struggles.

However, instead of letting this dishearten me, it fuelled a fire within. It became a catalyst for proving not just to him, but more importantly to myself, that success isn't solely defined by grades or conventional achievements. It's defined by resilience, determination, and the continuous pursuit of improvement.

This determination saw me through the initial and toughest years of entrepreneurship. I learned that while I might not have excelled in academic environments, I thrived in real world situations where strategy, people skills, and adaptability was key. My approach to recruitment mirrors this realisation, recognising each individual's unique potential beyond just their qualifications, championing our clients' growth, offering support and bespoke training solutions, and continuously evolving our methods to stay competitive.

Our unconventional approach has garnered more than just client satisfaction and successful placements; it has earned us industry recognition. Each award and accolade are a testament to our innovative methods' effectiveness and impact. These awards hold special significance, as they are not merely symbols of achievement, but poignant reminders of the challenges surmounted and the positive impact we've had on lives. Particularly noteworthy is our recognition by the very candidates we placed, a unique honour in an industry typically dominated by peer evaluations. This distinction, especially as we weren't competing against other agencies but against in-house teams, underscores our unique impact on the lives of individuals we've worked with.

Such recognition is a tribute to the collective effort of the K.A.G. team. It acknowledges the trust placed in us by candidates and the value our clients see in a different approach to recruitment. These awards symbolise a journey that began with a personal desire to innovate but has flourished thanks to a shared belief in the value of these differences. It's one that continues to evolve, propelled by our commitment to redefine the standards of the recruitment industry.

The Innovation of K.A.G.: Making a Mark

At K.A.G. Recruitment Consultancy, we've carved a distinctive track in the Recruitment industry. Founded in 2017, the business is a manifestation of my personal mission to shake up the status quo and address the complacency I have witnessed in the recruitment world. With a background deeply rooted in Recruitment from an early age, I started this business not from a place of financial abundance but fueled by a profound determination to bring about change.

Over the years, my commitment to infusing passion and hard work into the business has remained unwavering. K.A.G is not just another Recruitment firm; we're pioneers in changing how the world perceives recruitment. Our approach is rooted in understanding and aligning with the aspirations and visions of both clients and candidates. It's not just about making successful placements; it's about creating lasting relationships and ensuring the recruitment process is as fulfilling and impactful as possible.

With a collective experience of over 40 years in the field, our team at K.A.G. understands the nuances of recruitment like no other. We're known for our efficient, pain-free process, direct approach, and our ability to match the right candidate with the right business swiftly. Our straightforward, practical approach has been a refreshing change for our clients and candidates, a fact that's reflected in the numerous 5-star reviews and testimonials we've received.

THE RISE OF THE FEMALE ENTREPRENEUR

I firmly believe in the power of recruitment as a transformative tool for businesses. It's not just about filling a vacancy; it's about understanding the profound impact the right person in the right place can have. That's why we view each placement as a mission to strengthen the fabric of the organisations we work with.

As a fully remote business, we've embraced flexibility and adaptability as core principles. This allows us to cater to our clients' and candidates' needs more effectively, operating beyond the constraints of the traditional 9-5 workday. We specialise in a range of sectors, including Engineering, Manufacturing, IT, and Logistics, and cover a diverse range of roles within these areas, ensuring we can provide expert support no matter the requirement.

In building K.A.G., my vision extended beyond establishing a mere business; it was about cultivating a community where like-minded professionals could thrive on a commitment to excellence. Every interaction with clients and candidates is more than a transaction; it's about fostering partnerships that are geared towards long-term success and mutual growth. The foundation of K.A.G. is built on core values that are not just words to us but the principles we live and work by every day: Knowledge, Passion, Integrity, Trustworthiness, and Endurance.

These values are the pillars of K.A.G. and are critical to our business. They guide our actions, shape our culture, and define our identity in the marketplace. They are not just important; they are essential to who we are and everything we aspire to be.

As we move forward, the K.A.G. guarantee remains our commitment to delivering a seamless service you can trust. We back our words with action, ensuring peace of mind and profitable growth for your business. Whether you're a business seeking exceptional talent or a candidate looking for your next career opportunity, we're here to support, guide, and celebrate with you every step of the way.

From Interviews to Empowerment: By Your Side

My purpose in recruitment has been to bring a human touch back into an industry often criticised for being transactional, cold, and impersonal. It's about recognising the person behind each resume and the culture behind each company and Hiring Manager. Within this, I saw an opportunity to extend our offerings beyond the traditional recruitment services. Thus, venturing out several years ago into coaching and training, a natural extension that has allowed us to support both individuals and organisations in achieving their full potential.

The expansion into coaching and training was deliberate and thoughtful. It began with identifying the gaps and needs within the industry—where candidates were falling short through lack of support, what skills employers were seeking, and how we could bridge this divide. We started with Attraction and Interview Training, Leadership and communication workshops, which quickly gained traction and encouraged by this success, we expanded our repertoire to include specialised training in various industry skills and personal development training. Our approach was holistic, focusing not just on the technical skills, but also on the softer, often overlooked aspects of professional growth, such as emotional intelligence, resilience, and strategic thinking.

While recruitment remains at the core of our business, our expanded services are about bringing the best of both worlds to our clients. We understand that effective recruitment is not just about placing a candidate; it's about representing the company's ethos through its managers, providing candidates with a memorable interview experience, and supporting successful onboarding. Our involvement doesn't end with a candidate's placement; it extends to ensuring their integration and success within the new role. This is achieved through regular reviews at 3- and 6-month intervals with every candidate we place.

Aligning with clients and candidates has always been at the core of our recruitment practice, and this became even more crucial as we expanded our services. We've worked closely with clients to understand their long-term goals, company culture, and the specific challenges they face. This deep understanding allows us to tailor our coaching programs to suit their unique needs, ensuring that the training is not just relevant, but also impactful.

This comprehensive approach has significantly contributed to our impressive 92% retention rate. It reflects our understanding that successful recruitment is a journey, not a destination. By providing continuous support and training, we ensure that managers are well-equipped to represent their organisations effectively, and candidates are not only prepared for their roles but continue to grow and thrive within them. Our dual focus on recruitment and training ensures that we deliver a seamless, end-to-end service that benefits both our clients and candidates, fostering long-term success and satisfaction. This holistic approach has been a key driver in our growth and success, cementing our position as a leader in the recruitment industry, where we bring together the best services for all involved.

Looking ahead to 2024, one of my primary goals is to obtain my mBIT Coaching certification, and I am so excited to start this next step. This certification is not just a personal milestone; it's a strategy move to enhance the quality and breadth of our coaching services. mBIT is a powerful but simple coaching modality that blends Neuroscience, Positive Psychology, NLP, ancient wisdom and behavioural modelling together to bring about alignment and integration between a persons multiple brains, (head, heart & gut) in order to make wiser decisions. By harnessing the insights gained through mBIT, we can facilitate more meaningful growth and development, both for individuals seeking career advancement and organisations aiming to foster a more dynamic and cohesive workforce.

This certification also aligns with our broader vision for the future—to continue evolving, expanding, and excelling in what we do. We're committed to staying ahead of the curve, anticipating the changing needs of the industry, and continuously enhancing our services to meet and exceed these needs.

Our innovative 'By Your Side' service is further revolutionising our approach to recruitment. It's born from a commitment to be there for candidates every step of the way, particularly those in pursuit of their dream jobs who might need that extra bit of guidance and support. We understand that the journey to the perfect job isn't always straightforward. That's why we're here to assist with crafting standout CVs, compelling cover letters, and mastering interviews, even if we aren't acting as their primary recruiter. Our goal is to extend a helping hand to all who need it, embodying our belief that everyone deserves the chance to excel in their career path.

Beyond the Jobs: Family and Foundation

My family has been a cornerstone of support and inspiration. Their role has been multifaceted as motivators, sounding boards, and sometimes, the much-needed grounding force amongst the tumultuous world of business. Their unwavering belief in my vision has been a constant course of strength, propelling me forward even during the most challenging times and I am so grateful to have such a loving and supportive family, my husband being there every step of the way and having the ability to provide our son with an amazing life. This is absolutely priceless.

The sacrifices that come with building and growing a business weren't just mine to bear; my family lived them too. The long hours, the financial unpredictability, and the blurred lines between work and home life—they felt it all. Yet, their resilience and shared belief in me and the end goal turned these challenges into a collective mission. They've been right beside me, understanding the significance of our work and embracing the entrepreneurial journey as their own.

Their contribution to the business extends far beyond moral support. They've been involved in brainstorming sessions, decision-making, and at times, stepping in wherever needed. This collective effort has transformed our business into a genuine family endeavour, enriching it with diverse perspectives and a united vision. The sense of pride we share in what we've built together is profound, reflected not only in our professional achievements but in the deeper bonds and rich experiences we've shared along the way.

Naturally, embarking on this path raised eyebrows and doubts among some observers. Questions about the wisdom of entrepreneurship, blending family and business, and the feasibility of our ambitions were not uncommon. However, rather than diminishing our spirit, these doubts only strengthened our resolve. Each challenge became an opportunity to prove our commitment and capacity to succeed, reinforcing our collective belief in what we were building.

The value of our family business extends far beyond the conventional measures of success. It lies in the shared adventure, the collective growth, and the enduring values that we've nurtured together. It's about the support, understanding, and resilience that have become the hallmarks of our family's approach to business and life. Looking back at the trek so far, and ahead to what's yet to come, I'm grateful for the unwavering support and excited for the future chapters we'll write together. Our story is more than a business venture; it's proof of what can be achieved when you combine vision with a supportive family unit.

And to those who doubted my vision, thank you. Your scepticism became my fuel, turning doubts into determination. Each challenge you posed strengthened my resolve and taught me the value of believing in my path, no matter how unconventional it seemed. Your doubts kept me grounded, reminding me that true innovation often meets resistance. So, here's to the sceptics – you unknowingly played a part in my journey, and for that, I am grateful.

A Call to Collaborative Success: Our Story Together

My chapter is far from over. It continues as an earnest to growth, learning, and collective progress. This is why I invite you—whether you're an emerging entrepreneur, a forward-thinking organisation, or an individual keen on professional development—to join this ongoing journey. Let's unite to effect meaningful change in recruitment, constructing avenues of success and fostering environments that empower.

Reach out to share your narrative, ambitions, and ideas. Let's discover how our collaboration can set the stage for breakthroughs and innovation. The potential for your next significant opportunity is just a dialogue away. Together, let's step into a future where everyone's capabilities are fully realised, and every organisation achieves its vision.

Your story intertwines with ours; let's make it count.

Email: info@kagrecruitmentconsutlancy.co.uk
Website: www.kagrecruitmentconsultancy.co.uk
Website: www.theofficialkategerald.co.uk
@theofficialkategerald
@kagrecruitmentconsultancy
LinkedIn: www.linkedin.com/company/kagrecruitmentconsultancy
LinkedIn: www.linkedin.com/in/kate-gerald-recruitment

Special Offer: Just for You

As a special offering to everyone reading this book, I'm excited to share my Candidate Handbook. This comprehensive guide is my gift to you, a resource meticulously crafted to assist you in landing your dream job. It's a compilation of invaluable insights and practical advice, covering all the essentials from acing interviews to crafting compelling CVs and cover letters.

Email me to request your copy of the Candidate Handbook and take the first step towards securing your dream job with expert guidance.

Email: kate@kagrecruitmentconsultancy.co.uk

CHAPTER 22
Linda Scerri
Business Mentor | Certified Coach | Affiliate Marketer

In and out of The Ditch

On a cold, dark day in December 2019, in a small Worcestershire town called Redditch (quite literally a "red ditch" due to the red clay of the nearby River Arrow), a colleague at work asked me if I was tidying up my desk. I nodded, but little did she (or I) know that I was, in fact, gathering all my belongings, walking out of the office, my job and my 20+ year corporate career, never to return.

That year had seen me go from high-flying flavour of the month, Senior Sales

& Marketing Manager in a global manufacturing company, with sole responsibility for £30m of accounts, to seemingly not being able to add two and two together. As a single mum of 3 and sole income earner, I'd always been a "doer". I regularly used to fly to France for client meetings, all while running a home, organising school and childcare and looking after my elderly parents (one who was suffering from Alzheimer's and the other with a frail heart). When people say, "I don't know how you coped", I always think "I don't even know how I coped!!". I loved my job and flew through promotion after promotion, becoming known as "The Persuader" - someone who always got the best outcome for the company and the clients - but a re-structure in 2018 had resulted in redundancies, and although my role was safe, the tasks, actions, accounts and responsibilities of those who had left, were passed on to me, and it was about to get a whole heap worse.

My work bestie was promoted to become my manager. Once she got stuck into her new role, she became the proverbial rottweiler with me, and nothing I did was ever good enough. She was dedicated to her career, but being single with no kids, I'm not entirely convinced she had any empathy for those who were not on a similar career trajectory as her, and it became apparent that I was her number one target. Every passing day saw her tear my work apart, and this was on the back of going through the heartache of losing a second sister to cancer earlier that same year. I remember writing a text message to a friend saying I'd been awake half of the night dreaming how my ex-work-bestie-now-boss was tracking my every move – what a nightmare! If I had to sum up how I felt at work back then, I'd say it was like having a permanent fuzziness in my brain, and I felt like I was living one second behind myself. I now know that was stress and grief all bundled up into one big fat messy ball of messiness, but I didn't see it happening. I was putting on a brave face, but then the universe stepped in and stopped me in my tracks.

Just days after I'd walked out of my job, I moved into a dream country home with my partner. We'd been together four years, and the excitement of our first Christmas together in our first home was magical, but I woke up on Christmas morning to find he'd left me. Not only had he gone without me knowing during the night, he'd taken the turkey, the alcohol, the tea, coffee, sugar, mugs, television, Wi-Fi, radio and everything we needed to host Christmas day with my family! My friends and children rallied around, and we laughed when my sister had to drink a cup of tea out of the only recipient available – a gravy jug – but it really capped my annus horribilus and life as I knew it was over. No job, no dream home, no partner, and I was left wondering how I'd got here at the ripe old age of 55.

And worse still, the events of 2020 were about to unfold.

How a frog opened my eyes to entrepreneurship

At 16 and being a bit of a free-spirited but studious rebel, I left school and studied French at college, and it's here that I met my (future) French husband. Quite hilariously, after my first French lesson at school, I'd told my mum that I would marry a French man, and so it was that we got together on my 18th birthday and at 19, I moved lock, stock, and barrel to be with him in the south of France. We married when I was 21, and despite all my longing to be my own boss, I ended up working as a civil servant (silent groan) and living and working in France proved to be both the most wonderful experience and the most painful of times too. Turns out that leaving your country, home, family, working in a foreign country, speaking a foreign language, living with someone for the first time, and navigating adulthood is a lot to throw at a 19-year-old!

French life was wholesome; they certainly had a way of capitalising on a "slow-down" living that I absorbed. It's where we had our three children, where I discovered a love for all things food and health-related and interestingly, where I first found the wonderful world of shabby chic, which was later to become quite instrumental in my foray into working for myself. Family life was wonderful, but it was also horrendously difficult working shifts while bringing up small children, so I changed my role to be more of a 9-5 one and was happy-ish. "La Vie est Belle", as the French say.

But I missed England and my family desperately – ALL THE TIME – so when my husband's family business went under, we took the huge decision to move back to the UK, and so, having no jobs or home to go to as yet, we closed the French chapter of our lives and moved "home" just as I was turning 36.

Back in England, yet again, I fell into the 9-5 rat race with a global French company, and the pressure of having to "do – it – all" in terms of family, work and home took its toll, and my marriage fell apart. There I was, back in my beloved homeland, a single parent of three and still on the proverbial hamster wheel.

I soldiered on, but my job was an hour away from home, and so I quickly moved closer to home, starting as a French speaking customer service manager and was quickly promoted to French Account Manager, then Senior Sales & Marketing Manager, juggling tenders, teenage tantrums at home, life the universe and a bloomin' cherry on the top. If truth be told, a lot of it was done on autopilot, and yet I didn't have the head space, or the oomph needed to make any changes.

What I did do however, was carry on with the upcycling and restoration of furniture, and it really was the start of my entrepreneur era. It taught me so much about connections, cash and continuing to put one foot in front of the other to get to where I wanted to be. But where exactly did I want to be? That was the million-dollar question.

I spent any spare time I had (mostly on flights or in between business meetings) immersed in personal and professional development books, and that rekindled in me a love of all things brain-related. When my boss offered me the opportunity to train in a business modality that I could then roll out to the company, I leapt at the chance to stealth myself away from corporate tenders, excel sheets, statistics and data and that period formed the basis of a huge personal and professional shift.

It's here that my story gets messy as I engross myself in dreams of quitting corporate and working for myself, but as the saying goes: Nothing Changes If Nothing Changes.

Deja poo and the irony of the word entrepreneur being French

As the youngest of 6, you'd think I would have been spoiled, but I was very independent and grabbed every opportunity that was presented to me during my childhood, whether that was acting, singing, dancing, writing, sports or travelling.

My brain was constantly pinging with ideas of things I wanted to do "when I'm older" and being my own boss was never far from my thoughts. And so, as 2020 rolled around and I was out of a job, single and back at my home after splitting with my partner, and while others were seemingly slowing down during global lockdowns, I decided to take stock and invest in myself and my future business self, once and for all.

I went for it BIG TIME! I took a shed load of courses, paid mentors to guide me, gained qualifications and studied hard but hand on heart, nothing felt right. Yet I carried on learning about business strategy, SEO, copywriting, social media... you name it, I took a course on it. I joined groups, memberships, networked like a MOFO, listened to podcasts, and read blogs. I filled out oodles of workbooks, signed up for freebies, and sent myself voice notes galore. I had saved links, umpteen notebooks full of ideas, and thousands upon thousands of screenshot references, and while I found comfort in an online world that excited me, I just couldn't find the golden nugget. I wanted something that I felt passionate about, something that people wanted AND something that people would pay for, and whilst I could have done any number of things, nothing really lit me up and finding "my thing" proved elusive. Pretty pathetic for a 50+ woman who had always dreamt of being her own boss.

What would light me up? How could I combine my favourite things with what I was good at? What was I even good at, great at even? At this point in the story, I bet you're hoping that I had that lightbulb moment and found my dream future, but the famous saying "The More Things Change, The More Things Stay The Same" came to bite me on the bum, and I changed nothing. I carried on learning and I hate to admit it, but I watched with envy as others flew ahead with their dream entrepreneurial choices, and I had to face the harsh fact that I was dabbling when I should have been "doing".
Sure, I put myself out there. I created a large following on social media. Thousands joined my Facebook group. I was on podcasts and radio shows, I was in the National Press twice, and even in Best magazine with a double page

spread and featured on the front cover, and still I couldn't pin down what I wanted to do.

The irony wasn't lost on me that the word "entrepreneur" comes from the French verb "entreprendre"; to undertake. There I bloomin' well was undertaking all the things and yet still not being the business owner I wanted to be. Shut the front door, but that annoyed me and probably everyone around me. I flip-flopped (or Philippe – Philopped to keep the French theme going) time and time again, exhausting myself in the process.

Was it a mindset thing?
Was it a deep-rooted block I had?
Was I just not cut out for being an entrepreneur?
Was it that time a teacher had told me to "stop showing off?" (how I wish it had been because that would have been easy to address!)

Nope - the harsh reality was there was only ever me holding myself back and I wondered if I was ever going to figure "it" out. So, without a cat in hell's chance of figuring it out, I decided on a different tactic.

Cutting back just didn't cut it for me

Walking out of my career had been a no-brainer. I would have lost the last tiny bit of myself had I stayed in corporate. My big fat salary, 5-figure yearly bonuses, and pay-out when I left (hey, being on a three-month notice period and not having to work it had its advantages!) were all lovely but wouldn't last me forever, and so I rekindled my love affair with all things homey and became a bit of a prepper and super frugal mama.

I already knew how to cook from scratch, and I quickly discovered the world of homesteading. I fell head over heels in love with preserving food, canning it, dehydrating it, and freeze-drying it. I embraced growing my own vegetables, exchanging runner beans for apples with friends I'd made in my community. I cut back at home, making my own laundry powder and household cleaners, even making my own toothpaste.

I'd remembered all things low tox from my time in France, and at a time when people were shielding from the world and a deadly virus, I chose to build my immune system, increase connections, and delve into the world of being self-sufficient. I couldn't comprehend how the human race was meant to live if we slowly removed all connections to others and nature, so I went hell for leather into my Amish Era (think Laura Ingalls if you're old enough to remember Little House On The Prairie) and so it was that I recycled, re-used, re-invented, re-purposed, refurbished, repaired and re-thought how I wanted life to be. I truly believed that cutting back was the way to go. Not only because, as a nation, we tend to overconsume anyway, but it felt kinder to the planet to waste less. I wasn't wrong, but there was a flaw in my plan; a fly in my ointment.

My eldest son had moved to Australia permanently in 2016, and I missed him dreadfully. In 2023, my 25-year-old daughter (my youngest and who was still living with me) decided she wanted to move to Australia to spend some time with her brother. I knew there was a real possibility of her falling in love with the country (or falling in love full stop), and so now I was faced with the real possibility of having two-thirds of my children living on the other side of the world and no money to visit them regularly, and that broke me inside.
Well, there's nothing like having a fire lit up under your belly to spur you on and scare the living daylights out of you. The thought of not being in their lives haunted me but also made me laser focussed on finding a solution, and I came

to the realisation that it couldn't come from being a modern-day Jack and The Beanstalk, trading a cow for a bag of beans, no matter how magical they were!

At that very same time, I happened to notice a friend I'd followed online metamorphosize into being an entrepreneur extraordinaire. Not only was she doing it seamlessly, she was also brilliant at talking about it, and I was intrigued.

What if I could do what she was doing?
What if I gave up cutting back and instead invested one last time?
What if this was the golden nugget I'd been waiting for all these years?
What if this was my ticket to a life of freedom, travel and income?
What if this was the gateway out of the hustle and grind and what had I got to lose?

I'm nothing if not curious and so I contacted her to find out whether this was, in fact, pie in the sky or the magical bean I'd been dreaming of since I was a little girl.

Finally finding my groove

"Whoah, Whoah, Whoah. Hold on a minute Linda. Your chapter is peppered with stories of you messing about and fluffing things up. You don't really expect us to believe that your journey to entrepreneurship happened just like magic, do you?"

Well, I'd love to say I'm now a 7-figure biz owner, working just 2 hours a day from my phone on some tropical island, but a) I'm a country bumpkin at heart and don't even like the beach and b) we all know those kind of stories (even if some are real) are few and far between. I know it might be hard to believe that the universe handed me the right opportunity at the right time, but it's true, and I'd say it was about bloomin' time!

I'd just cashed in my pension and was looking to invest some of it. Should I invest in stocks and shares? I knew nothing about them. Gold? Maybe, but you can't really melt it down when you need an airline ticket! Crypto? Definitely not my cup of tea. Nothing felt right, so I put all of my focus and energy into really, REALLY asking myself what I truly wanted, and that was a simple online business so I could be at home AND earn enough money to get to see my children in Australia whenever I wanted, for as long as I wanted. I didn't want to do it alone, but I didn't want a business partner. I wanted it to be in the wellness industry, but I didn't want it to be in the low-ticket beauty arena. I wanted it to be scalable but not lead to burnout. I wanted it to be something I could share with others, and I wanted my return on investment to happen fast.

I wasn't asking much, was I? (I'd put a few LOL emojis here if I could because trust me when I say I knew I was asking for the moon on a stick). And so it was that I saw that post my online friend had put up on social media. We arranged to have a chat, and I got to hear about an amazing, no-brainer business model and the earth-loving flagship product she couldn't stop talking about, and I realised that I could do it too. I remember thinking (and more importantly, feeling) that this was it. This was the golden effin' nugget I'd been waiting for.

I knew that I had always had everything I needed to succeed, but I also knew I would probably never do it alone, so it reassured me that this opportunity came with an online community, support, mentorship, systems, automations, and the chance to scale by leveraging social media with me being my own brand. The 9-year-old performer in me was doing cartwheels!

I'm a numbers girl (a throwback to my corporate days spent with ten billion tabs open on multiple spreadsheets making money for someone else to live their dream), and once I saw the commission structure, I couldn't unsee it so it was a full body HECK YES from me. I jumped into a wonderful community of warrior women (and men), all with a patented high-commission compensation plan, structured processes and "set and forget" systems.

Turns out the Linda of 2019 who quit the corporate hustle and grind; the Linda who wanted to do business in an aligned way; the Linda who understood the importance of community over competition; the Linda who craved a low-tox life and the Linda who wanted a high return for any investment might have just found the magic bean.

Turns out that the tears I had cried over the years had actually been watering the seeds I'd planted for 2024.

Linda Scerri
Live More – Earn More

Linktree: https://linktr.ee/lindascerri

"What we know matters but who we are matters more." Brené Brown

THE RISE OF THE FEMALE ENTREPRENEUR

CHAPTER 23
Sarah Makinde
Chartered Psychologist, Training Expert & Master Strengths Coach to HR Professionals, Psychologists and Coaches

From Tragedy to Triumph - How I Beat the Statistics

Statistically speaking, I shouldn't be where I am today. I was an immigrant from Nigeria. I was a teenage mum at the age of 18. I was a girl full of so much anxiety that she felt that her voice wasn't worth listening to by anyone. Yet here I am today. Collaborating with 22 other amazing women, sharing my story of tragedy, female entrepreneurship and triumph - how is this possible?

Like the great athlete, Kareem Abdul-Jabbar said: "You won't win until you learn how to lose". My story begins with learning how to lose in the biggest way. It's a story I haven't shared with many people before now, so here we go - no holds barred!

The Biggest Loss of My Life

Have you ever experienced loss? You know, the kind of loss that has you wondering if life will ever be the same again?

Well, in 2015, I experienced a loss like I had never experienced before. The loss hit me hard. Everything disappeared at that moment. I couldn't stop the tears and the heartache. I thought we would have more time together. I wasn't ready to say goodbye. People kept telling me I would get over it and the pain would lessen in time. I kept saying it wouldn't. The loss had left a hole in my life. One that I never thought would be filled again.

This was the day I lost what I thought was my everything - it felt tragic. It was the loss of something that was so dear to me - my job! You might laugh, or feel shocked by this drastic statement, but this wasn't just a job to me. This was my identity, the thing that gave my life meaning, my passion, and my future, all wrapped into one.

Believe it or not, there were over 100,000 people made redundant in the three months to June 2023 in just the UK, according to The Office of National Statistics (ONS, 2023). Redundancy in some form or another, will have touched the lives of many people you know. This loss of a job, as the mental health charity Mind states, can impact people in different ways - ranging from a sense of shock to a lack of uncertainty, or even to a sense of acceptance.

For me, the loss of my job felt unbearable. It felt like the end of everything. My job was the symbol of everything I had worked so hard to achieve as an immigrant who was looked down on by society, as a teen mum who was cast aside by the majority of people around me, and as someone who didn't believe they would amount to anything much in life because of her own limiting beliefs and feeling like an imposter.

What made the redundancy worse was that it felt like the loss was out of my hands. I was in the middle of a mental health crisis - panic attacks, overwhelm and anxiety. I had to end my job and opt for redundancy, or ultimately, I felt this would lead to the end of me!

I didn't know it at the time, but it was the loss of this corporate job that would change the course of my life as I knew it. It was this loss that would lead onto a much more fulfilling path, which ultimately would lead to the start of my business journey. Little did I know in this pit of total despair, it would be this breakdown that would lead me to my breakthrough. It was this ending that would make room for a new beginning.

Now let me take you even further back to be able to take you further forwards…

Where It All Began

I was born in humble surroundings - a city in Nigeria, Jos. From the African plains, we moved to the Yorkshire dales - we had very little at that time. We had just enough money for the rent and food, but not enough money for life's luxuries and keeping up with all the trends. I was envious of my school friends and longed for the life I saw them living. Their holidays, their beautiful homes, their rooms full of the latest toys. They were living the life I could only dream of.

I didn't know I was different, until the difference became all I knew. The comparisons consumed my mind every day. Feelings of being less than everyone around me just became my way of life. It felt normal to put everyone on a pedestal and constantly look up, wishing I could be where they were. No, it was more than that. I found myself wishing I could be who they were and not who I was. I didn't want to be me.

My childhood didn't last long when I left home at 15 and soon became a teen mum at 18. I had to grow up fast. If I thought I couldn't afford the luxuries and I was different before, this feeling multiplied tenfold when I became a teenage mum.

Memories stay ingrained in my mind of running to the toilet to be sick whilst studying for my A-levels. Worrying about being able to afford gas, electricity, and food. Memories of comparing my nights in, feeling trapped with worry as my only company, with my friends and their nights out at the prom, feeling carefree and young.

Becoming a teen mum meant I soon became a statistic. Surrounded by the negative stigma of having a baby whilst studying for my A-levels. Faced with constant judgement by society and assumptions that I wasn't going to achieve much, if anything, in life. I felt lower than I had ever felt before.

Sadly, this is not unusual. Teen mothers are routinely seen as having physical, psychological, mental, emotional, and social problems and as being poor parents. Many people assume teen mothers are troubled and dependent. These negative stereotypes people hold about young mothers mean they are more likely to become pregnant again quite soon after their first child and not progress in education (Psychology Today, 2023).

Over the next few years with working, studying, caring for my son, and struggling financially, my mind grew tired, and my body grew weary, but I kept going on this rollercoaster of a ride. Determined to beat the statistics. I wasn't doing it just for me anymore, I had to make a better life for my little boy.

The Moment Of My Breakdown

For years, the momentum and adrenaline (and caffeine!) kept me going. As I entered the corporate world straight from university after completing my Masters with my young son by my side, I tried to hide my past out of fear of more judgement. I didn't share much about my background or tell anyone about where I had been as a young mum. I only talked about where I wanted to go in my career. With big dreams of promotions and climbing the career ladder - I had visions of living the corporate dream.

I can't say if I enjoyed my life at that time, all I know is that I still didn't enjoy being me at that time. Once again, but this time at work, I felt like I was different and didn't fit in. Held back by scars from my past struggles and my harsh internal critic. Life felt hard. The deep wounds, and low self esteem were patched up by the compliments for the work produced and being praised for my work ethic. These highs on the outside, felt, at the time, like they more than compensated for the lows on the inside.

It became addictive - doing more and more to get the praise from others that I couldn't and didn't know how to give to myself. Little did I know that in reality,

I was drowning. I couldn't see and wasn't expecting what was coming - this was the moment I had my breakdown!

All I remember was being taken into a corner of the office shaking uncontrollably. The floodgate of tears had opened, and there was nothing that could have held them back. I was having a breakdown. I was in the middle of a mental health crisis.

Think of four people you know. The sad fact is that one in every four of these people in the UK will experience a mental health problem each year (Mind, 2023). I was fast becoming part of another statistic. But once again, I knew that this was another statistic that I wouldn't let dictate the rest of my life.

The day I left the corporate office, the day I walked down those stairs, the day I stepped out of that door, the day I gave up my job. Whilst it felt like the end of my life as I knew it. I knew that this wasn't the end of my story. There was much more still to come.

The Moment Of My Breakthrough

The grief I felt over the next few months was unimaginable. Several weeks of living in limbo, panic attacks, waking up not being able to catch my breath. Fear of failure, fear of financial lack, fear of the unknown.

Despite this experience, I found my mind wanting to keep me 'safe' and take me back to what felt familiar. But I knew that I would just end up here again. In this same situation, feeling deep inside me like I wasn't enough. Like I didn't matter - defective and different. Wishing I was anyone but myself. Yet again!

The darkness went on for months. It was like I was in hibernation. Locked away from the world, not knowing if I was in a dream or wide awake. It was in these months of despair that, with just enough energy to get through the days, I found joy in learning new things. I fell in love with self development, mindfulness, Neurolinguistic programming (NLP) and positive psychology. In learning ways to help myself, I found ways in which I could help others who might be going through a similar experience of not feeling they are good enough.

Like a metamorphosis and breaking myself down on a cellular level in order to rebuild. I could feel that things were changing. I began to take a different perspective and change the lens through which I was viewing my world - not just with work but also with my personal life.

When I had space to heal the inside, I had time to begin to look at the outside. It's like I started to see my life and my journey to this point with more clarity, and with much more kindness to myself, to others, and to my circumstances.

I know now that I had to let go of everything I thought I was to become and who I had the potential to be.

Over the next few years, I learned more about business and how to set up my own company and services. I leveraged the opportunities around me with my existing property that I bought when I was in my 20s to become a landlady, to grow this business further, turning it into a successful property portfolio. I now have five properties, including holiday lettings, serviced accommodation, HMO's and short-term lettings. These are a mixture of both privately and jointly owned houses. I also love getting involved in the planning of house renovations, and I am so passionate about turning properties into businesses with as much equity as possible.

I invested in over 50,000 hours of education and training in psychology, mindfulness, hypnotherapy, NLP, strengths coaching and more. I then decided to expand my love of these various modalities that had saved my own life, into the growth of my own coaching, consulting and training business - Eight Academy. I now help other HR professionals, Psychologists, and Coaches create additional streams of income, grow their businesses, and increase their impact. This in turn, helps them raise their prices, stand out in their niche market and have more freedom to live life on their own terms.

Fast forward to today, and along with my property and eight academy businesses, I not only completed my degree and masters as a teen mum, I more recently went on to complete my second masters in Human Resource Management and my Doctorate Level Chartership in Occupational Psychology, to become recognised now as an HCPC Registered Chartered Psychologist!

Who would have guessed so much could happen in just a few years?

The Difference That Made The Difference

Now, you might read my story and think that everything has been plain sailing since my breakthrough and starting my businesses. Not at all! I have since experienced many setbacks and challenges. The point of me telling you this story isn't to paint a picture of the 'easy' life of a female entrepreneur, the glamour and the glitz. It's to show the reality of life and to share the lessons that have really helped me. In the hope this will make the difference to someone else out there.

With that in mind, let me share just some of the golden nuggets I've picked up along the way.

Have you ever watched a movie for the second time? You might see things that you perhaps didn't see before. Even going as far to say it creates a whole new meaning to the story. Here's my story again - this time offering a different perspective, now that I have been able to connect the dots looking back and see why it all happened as it did:

Golden Nugget Number 1: Being present and practising gratitude can change our perspective of our current circumstances. There is always something to be grateful for. All my life, I didn't realise that I was focusing on my humble beginnings, my disadvantages as a teenage mum, my redundancy and loss. What I didn't focus on was the opportunities, the achievements and the progress. I always thought I became abundant after my breakdown and my redundancy. But what I couldn't see then is the fact that I was already abundant, even before I was made redundant.

Golden Nugget Number 2: We don't have to live with the label we are given, or that we may have given ourselves. The statistics don't need to be our story. We can use attempts to disempower as opportunities and motivation to empower. We can become who we were made to be, not who we were told to be. Yes, I was a teenage mum, but when I was focusing on the struggles, the stigma and being different to my peers, I wasn't focused on my determination, motivation and how I was achieving so much with so very little.

Golden Nugget Number 3: Our story can be our glory. What we think is a failure can turn into our fuel for success. Our losses can become our wins. They become the words that we carry forwards to inspire generations to come. Absolutely no one else can tell our own story better than we can. It's time to get visible and share our journey!

It has taken me years to stop being ashamed of my past and to tell my story including all the ups and downs. However, I realise now that there is power in my story and my own journey. By embracing where I have come from, I can help other people get where they want to go through what I do in my business.

Now, let me leave you with the following key question: How can you use your own story and journey so far to inspire others and help them get to where they want to be in business and in life?

"Life is full of rollercoaster moments - embrace the ride. It's only when you look back that you realise every high and low was exactly as it was meant to be. It will all make sense, the dots will connect at the most unexpected times. When the dots do connect, be prepared to have one heck of an inspiring story to share" - Sarah Makinde (2023)

If you enjoyed my story, let's get connected:

Website: www.eightacademy.com
Facebook: www.facebook.com/thecharteredpsychologist
Instagram: www.instagram.com/thecharteredpsychologist
LinkedIn: www.linkedin.com/in/sarahmakinde

ACKNOWLEGEMENTS

Thankyou to Lyndsey Meredith for making this book possible, and for getting together these amazing ladies to share their stories and inspire each and everyone of us.

Thank you to everyone who have supported us and helped us raise money for the prices trust charity.

As a collective we would like to thank Tracey Munro of Pro Publishing House for all of her help and support in the writing and publishing of this book. We definitely couldn't have done it without you!

Our chosen charity

All proceeds from this book will go to a charity that we have chosen as a collective. "Women Supporting Women" is a part of The Princes Trust and we felt that it was very aligned to our mission of inspiring and supporting other women to rise and achieve their own potential.

The mission of Women Supporting Women is simple: to nurture, empower and inspire young women to build a better future for themselves.

To find out more about Women Supporting Women and the amazing work that they do and to donate to them directly go to:

www.princes-trust.org.uk/support-our-work/major-gifts/women-supporting-women

THE RISE OF THE FEMALE ENTREPRENEUR

Printed in Great Britain
by Amazon